THE NORMANDY
CAMPAIGN, 1944

Bibliographies of Battles and Leaders

The Battle of Antietam and the Maryland Campaign of 1862: A
Bibliography
D. Scott Hartwig

The Central Pacific Campaign, 1943–1944: A Bibliography
James T. Controvich

American Warplanes 1908–1988: A Bibliography
Myron J. Smith, Jr.

Pearl Harbor: A Bibliography
Myron J. Smith, Jr.

The Battles of Coral Sea and Midway, 1942: A Selected Bibliography
Myron J. Smith, Jr.

The Battle of Jutland: A Bibliography
Eugene L. Rasor

The Falklands/Malvinas Campaign: A Bibliography
Eugene L. Rasor

THE NORMANDY CAMPAIGN, 1944

A Selected Bibliography

Colin F. Baxter

Bibliographies of Battles and Leaders, Number 9
Myron J. Smith, Jr., Series Editor

Greenwood Press
New York • Westport, Connecticut • London

Library of Congress Cataloging-in-Publication Data

Baxter, Colin F.
    The Normandy campaign, 1944 : a selected bibliography / Colin F.
Baxter.
        p.   cm.—(Bibliographies of battles and leaders, ISSN
1056-7410 ; no. 9)
    Includes index.
    ISBN 0-313-28301-X (alk. paper)
    1. World War, 1939-1945—Campaigns—France—Normandy—
Bibliography. 2. Normandy (France)—History—Bibliography.
I. Title. II. Series.
Z6207.W8B35 1992
[D756.5.N6]
016.94054'2142—dc20   91-46970

British Library Cataloguing in Publication Data is available.

Library of Congress Catalog Card Number: 91-46970
ISBN: 0-313-28301-X
ISSN: 1056-7410

First published in 1992

Greenwood Press, 88 Post Road West, Westport, CT 06881
An imprint of Greenwood Publishing Group, Inc.

Printed in the United States of America

The paper used in this book complies with the
Permanent Paper Standard issued by the National
Information Standards Organization (Z39.48-1984).

10 9 8 7 6 5 4 3 2 1

CONTENTS

PREFACE

This book, a volume in the Bibliographies of Battles and Leaders series, is intended to be a reference and research guide for the student, scholar, and general reader with an interest in one of the most decisive battles in history.

Part I, the heart of this bibliographical work, is an historiographical narrative that evaluates and critically reviews the literature on the Normandy campaign. My aim has been to integrate the multitude of books, articles, memoirs, and other materials that have been published on the Normandy campaign into a complete tapestry, thus making the battle understandable from a variety of perspectives. Chapter 8 offers some conclusions and suggestions for further research.

Part II of the book consists of an extensive, but selective, alphabetical listing of the leading and significant contributions to the writing on this epic battle. Citations are cross-referenced from the historiographical narrative in Part I to the alphabetical listing in Part II and vice versa.

I would like to extend a special thanks to the following individuals for their suggestions, encouragement, and assistance

in the writing of this bibliography: Correlli Barnett, Churchill
College Archives; Beth Hogan, Librarian, ETSU; Eugene Rasor,
Emory and Henry College; James Slonaker, Historical Reference
Branch, U. S. Army Military History Institute; Myron J. Smith,
Jr., series editor; David R. Woodward, Marshall University; and
my colleagues, Professors Ron Day and Stephen Fritz. Finally, I
would like to acknowledge the support, encouragement and
patience of my wife, Tamara, and son, Andrew, without whose
help this book would not have been possible.

PART I

NARRATIVE AND HISTORIOGRAPHICAL SURVEY

Chapter 1

HISTORICAL BACKGROUND

D-Day, June 6, 1944. All over the world the news is broadcast that the long-awaited invasion of Hitler's fortress Europe has begun. Allied forces have landed in Normandy. The liberation of Occupied Europe is at hand. A young Jewish girl in Amsterdam writes in her diary that this is *the* day! Friends are approaching, soon her family will be saved. In the Soviet Union, Stalin acknowledges the tremendous achievement of Allied armies crossing the Channel: "The history of war has never witnessed such a grandiose operation." In the United States, Britain, and Canada, and other Allied nations, millions of families anxiously await the outcome of the invasion. It is with good reason that historian Stephen Ambrose refers to D-Day as "the most important day of the 20th century."

The climax of all previous Allied actions against Nazism, D-Day is said to be the greatest feat of organization in human history. The combined planning of American and British staffs, working together as a single team, resulted in the precise execution of an operation so complicated that, in the words of General George C. Marshall, the American Chief of Staff, it "almost defies description." Two million troops of various nationalities, nearly 5,000 ships and 11,000 aircraft were assembled and organized without the enemy knowing where or when the assault would take place; all this in the days before computers and fully dependable communications systems.

Even with two-thirds of the German army pinned down in the Soviet Union, even with U.S. resources and manpower, the Normandy assault was far from a foregone conclusion. As British Prime Minister Winston Churchill warned, a disastrous defeat on the coast of France was "the only way in which we could possibly lose this war." At a briefing on June 6, Adolf Hitler chuckled in a carefree manner, behaving as if this was the opportunity he had been waiting for to settle accounts with his enemies. Heinz Guderian, the Inspector-General of the armored forces, had once said to Fritz Bayerlein, commander of the elite Panzer Lehr Division, "With this division alone you will throw the Anglo-Americans back into the sea. Into the sea." Guderian emphasized, "Remember. Your objective is not the coast but the sea." At Normandy, the ordinary German soldier fought with bravery and determination.

If the invasion succeeded, it would involve Hitler in a full-scale land war on a second major front; if the invasion failed, then Hitler would have been safe in the west for some time to come—time in which to develop the new submarines, the jet fighters and bombers, and other weapons on which Hitler pinned his hopes. Given the heavy strains on Anglo-American relations, an Allied defeat in Normandy might well have forced President Roosevelt to bow to pressure to give first priority to the war against Japan. Hitler might not have survived the war, but most of Europe, and not just the eastern half of it, would have been liberated by the Soviet Union.

Cornelius Ryan's justly famous book *The Longest Day*, published in 1959, and the 1964 film based on Ryan's book that starred virtually every famous actor and actress in Hollywood, created the image of D-Day as the climax of the war, with scenes of awesome Allied power—ships stretching for miles and fleets of aircraft. D-Day, however, was merely the prelude to a long drawn-out campaign in which gains were measured in terms of fields rather than miles. By the time of the American breakout at St. Lô at the end of July, the Allies had suffered 122,000 casualties while penetrating thirty miles deep into an eighty-mile front. D-Day was the first round in a battle that Rommel called "one terrible blood-letting."

A campaign prolific in controversies, C. P. Stacey, the official Canadian historian of the Battle of Normandy, declared that "Much nonsense has been talked and written about the Normandy landings, and the most foolish story of all is the legend that the operation was easy and almost bloodless." Could the Germans have won at Normandy? Historian Martin Blumenson has answered the question with a definite yes, arguing that the Germans could well have won. On the other hand, Martin van Creveld has wondered whether or not the Normandy campaign was not a "walk-over" after all. Debate over the Second Front question, the significance of air power, the role of intelligence and deception, Eisenhower's and Montgomery's generalship, tactics and personalities, the German response, and the fighting ability of Allied troops are just a few of the topics that have aroused heated controversy both at the time and in the years since 1944. Historians, like some of the participants in those great events, have aggravated and overemphasized some of the differences. To pretend that there were no bitter disputes, however, would be a travesty of the truth and make history worse than valueless—like the royal sundial that tells only of the "shining hours" of sweetness and light.

Nearly half a century has passed since D-Day. For those who participated in the epic event or remember World War II, June 6 is one of those never-to-be-forgotten dates in history. For a new generation of young people, those born since World War II, the Battle of Normandy belongs with Thermopylae, the Armada, Gettysburg, and Iwo Jima to a distant, yet treasured, past.

The Normandy countryside, with its small fields, high hedges, apple orchards and rolling hills (the famous bocage country), is one of the most beautiful parts of France. The beaches attract thousands of visitors each year. The abandoned gun emplacements, the monument to the Rangers at Pointe du Hoc and those to the airborne at Sainte Mere-Eglise and Pegasus Bridge, the quiet American cemetery at Colleville-sur-Mer overlooking Omaha Beach, the German cemetery at Cambe, and the British and Canadian graves on the road to Caen bear silent witness to the price that both victor and vanquished paid in one of the most decisive battles in world history. It decided the fate of Nazi Germany.

Chapter 2

SOURCES FOR RESEARCH ON THE NORMANDY CAMPAIGN

PRINCIPAL RESEARCH COLLECTIONS

Dwight D. Eisenhower Library, Abilene, Kansas

The Pre-Presidential Papers of General Eisenhower, who was appointed Supreme Commander of the Allied Expeditionary Force, in December 1943, contain his correspondence with the key figures in Operation OVERLORD. Many of these letters have been published in The Johns Hopkins Press volumes, THE PAPERS OF DWIGHT DAVID EISENHOWER: THE WAR YEARS, edited by Alfred D. Chandler, Jr. Volume 3 pertains to OVERLORD. Other sources include the diary of Harry C. Butcher, Eisenhower's naval aide; the Walter Bedell Smith papers, Eisenhower's Chief of Staff; the Harold R. Bull papers, appointed G-3 (Operations section) Supreme Headquarters Allied Expeditionary Force (SHAEF) in February 1944; the J. Lawton Collins papers, Commander VII Corps; the Norman D. Cota papers, Commander of the 28th Division; and an oral history transcript by Ray W. Barker, Deputy Chief of Staff to Supreme Allied Commander (COSSAC, Chief of Staff to the Supreme Allied

Commander) then Assistant Chief of Staff, G-1 (Personnel section), SHAEF. Under orders from General George C. Marshall, Barker joined British planners in 1942 who were working on plans for a cross-Channel attack. At the entrance to the Eisenhower Museum may be seen a D-Day mural. Eisenhower's hand-written note accepting responsibility, in the event of failure, for the invasion is among other items on display in this excellent museum.

United States Army Military History Institute, Carlisle Barracks, Pennsylvania

Omar N. Bradley papers, including the Chester A. Hansen (Bradley's aide) diary; the voluminous Reports of the General Board, U.S. Forces, European Theater; the Forrest C. Pogue interviews with the COSSAC planning staff; the German Report Series, manuscript interviews with high ranking German officers, many of whom were involved in the Normandy campaign. Initially, all the contributors were POW or internees; participation, however, was voluntary; U.S. Army unit histories; WORLD WAR II COMBAT INTERVIEWS (conducted by Army combat historians) on microfiche. Modern Military Branch, National Archives, Washington, D.C.

U.S. War Department records such as those of the Joint Chiefs of Staff; SHAEF/SGS (Secretary, General Staff); unit operational records are located at the National Records Center, Suitland, Maryland.

Manuscript Division, Library of Congress, Washington, D.C.

The papers of Henry H. (Hap) Arnold, Commanding General, Army Air Forces; Carl A. Spaatz papers, Commander U.S. Strategic Air Forces in Europe.

Naval Historical Center, Washington Navy Yard, Washington, D.C.

The operational archives section contains the action reports of U.S. naval vessels engaged in Operation NEPTUNE, the amphibious side of OVERLORD. The files of Samuel Elliot Morison contain material used in his HISTORY OF U.S. NAVAL OPERATIONS IN WORLD WAR II. Volume XI is the relevant volume for Operation NEPTUNE.

United States Air Force Historical Research Center, Maxwell Air Force Base, Montgomery, Alabama

Contains collections on the 9th Air Force, including records of squadrons, groups, and wings. Various records of SHAEF and British Air Ministry are also at the Center.

George C. Marshall Library/Archives, Virginia Military Institute, Lexington, Virginia

Various personal papers and official reports relating to the Normandy campaign.

Eisenhower Center, University of New Orleans, Louisiana

D-Day oral history collection. Director of the program, Stephen Ambrose (Eisenhower's biographer and author of PEGASUS BRIDGE, JUNE 6, 1944) has contributed the transcripts of his own interviews with many of the participants in D-Day. The Center is preparing audio cassettes of selections from the oral histories, and plans to publish them in time for the fiftieth anniversary in 1994.

Directorate of History, Department of National Defence and the National Archives of Canada, Ottawa, Canada

Army war diaries, historical officers' reports, and other unit information can be found in Record Group 24. General H.D.G. Crerar's papers (commander, 1st Canadian Army) are in the Manuscript Division. The files of the air force overseas headquarters in London, rich in Normany material, are at the Directorate of History. Many Canadian records are available on microfilm or microfiche.

Public Record Office, Kew, London

The records of the British 21st Army Group are found under WO (War Office) 205; SHAEF records, WO 219; unit war diaries, WO 168; narratives of medical units in action, WO 222; Operation NEPTUNE, ADM 199; operations of 2nd Tactical Air Force, AIR 27; many other planning and operations reports.

Churchill Archives Centre, Cambridge University, England

Churchill's own papers are presently closed to researchers, but other collections relating to the Normandy campaign include the Sir James Grigg papers, British Secretary of State for War; the Stephen Roskill papers, naval historian; the Admiral Bertram H. Ramsay papers, Allied Naval Commander in Chief, Expeditionary Force; and the Selwyn Lloyd papers, Deputy Chief of Staff, British Second Army.

Liddell Hart Centre for Military Archives, King's College, University of London

Includes Liddell Hart's own vast correspondence (Liddell Hart was one of the most influential military writers of the twentieth century), the Alanbrooke papers (Chief of the Imperial General Staff), the Ismay papers (Churchill's military advisor), the Francis de Guingand papers (Montgomery's Chief of Staff), the papers of Sir Miles Dempsey (Commander, British Second Army), and postwar interrogation reports of German generals.

The Imperial War Museum, London

Contains the papers of Field Marshal Bernard Law Montgomery who commanded the Allied assault forces in Normandy, serving in that capacity until September 1, 1944 when General Eisenhower assumed control of field operations; the papers of G. C. Bucknall, Commander, British XXX Corps; included in the Bucknall collection are his answers to Chester Wilmot's questions concerning XXX Corps operations in Normandy; the E. J. Kingston-McCloughry papers, SHAEF air planning staff; many other personal letters of participants in the Normandy campaign. Vast collection of photographs and sound recordings.

Militageschtlichen Forschungsamt (Military History Agency), Freiburg, Germany

Contains such items as the records of Army Group B (operational orders), naval and air records, situation reports, the Jodl diary, the diary of Air Force General Koller, and the correspondence of Von Schweppenburg.

Bibliotheque du Service Historique de l'Armee de Terre. Chateau de Vincennes, Vincennes, Paris

Together with the Archives historiques de guerre, Chateau de Vincennes, the library is an essential source for French military history.

Bibliotheque Historique de la Marine. Chateau de Vincennes, Vincennes, Paris

Special collection on naval history.

Bibliotheque Municipale, Caen

Special Normandy collection.

BIBLIOGRAPHIES AND GUIDES

Gwyn M. Bayliss. BIBLIOGRAPHIC GUIDE TO THE TWO WORLD WARS: AN ANNOTATED SURVEY OF ENGLISH-LANGUAGE REFERENCE MATERIALS. New York, 1978. [29]. A guide to the guides. The book attempts to describe the most important published reference aids available.

Keith W. Bird. GERMAN NAVAL HISTORY: A GUIDE TO THE LITERATURE. New York, 1985. [45].

Paolo Coletta. A BIBLIOGRAPHY OF AMERICAN NAVAL HISTORY. Annapolis, 1981. [101].

O. A. Cooke. THE CANADIAN MILITARY EXPERIENCE, 1867-1983: A BIBLIOGRAPHY. 2d ed. [106].

Charles E. Dornbusch. CANADIAN ARMY, 1855-1965: LINEAGES, REGIMENTAL HISTORIES [133].

Charles E. Dornbusch. UNIT HISTORIES, PERSONAL NARRATIVES, UNITED STATES ARMY: A CHECKLIST. A list of nearly 3,000 unit histories [134].

A. G. S. Enser. A SUBJECT BIBLIOGRAPHY OF THE SECOND WORLD WAR: BOOKS IN ENGLISH, 1939-1974 [154].

A. G. S. Enser. A SUBJECT BIBLIOGRAPHY OF THE SECOND WORLD WAR: BOOKS IN ENGLISH, 1975-1983 [155].

Arthur L. Funk. THE SECOND WORLD WAR: A SELECT BIBLIOGRAPHY OF BOOKS IN ENGLISH SINCE 1975. Claremont, Calif., 1985. [174].

Christopher R. Gabel. BOOKS ON OVERLORD: A SELECT BIBLIOGRAPHY AND RESEARCH AGENDA ON THE NORMANDY CAMPAIGN, 1944. Published in the journal MILITARY AFFAIRS (1984) [177].

Robin Higham. A GUIDE TO THE SOURCES IN AMERI-
CAN MILITARY HISTORY [230].
Robin Higham. A GUIDE TO THE SOURCES IN BRITISH
MILITARY HISTORY. Berkeley, Calif., 1971. [231].
Gerald Jordan. BRITISH MILITARY HISTORY: A SUPPLE-
MENT TO ROBIN HIGHAM'S GUIDE TO THE
SOURCES. New York, 1988. [261]. Contains 6,400
entries.
George S. Pappas. UNITED STATES ARMY UNIT HISTO-
RIES. Special bibliographic series No. 4. Carlisle Bar-
racks, PA., 1971. [379].
Eugene L. Rasor. BRITISH NAVAL HISTORY SINCE 1815.
A GUIDE TO THE LITERATURE. New York, 1990.
[397]. Contains a section on the Normandy invasion.
Revue d'Histoire de la Deuxieme Guerre Mondiale. Paris,
1950– . Most work in most languages on the Second
World War is noticed in the journal. Its name since 1987
is *Guerres mondiales et conflits contemporains*.
Dennis E. Showalter. GERMAN MILITARY HISTORY:
1648–1982: A CRITICAL BIBLIOGRAPHY. New
York, 1984. [437].
Myron J. Smith, Jr. WORLD WAR II: THE EUROPEAN
AND MEDITERRANEAN THEATERS. AN ANNO-
TATED BIBLIOGRAPHY. New York, 1984. [446].
Myron J. Smith, Jr. WORLD WAR II AT SEA: A BIBLIOG-
RAPHY OF SOURCES IN ENGLISH. VOL. 1 : THE
EUROPEAN THEATER. Metuchen, 1976. [447]. Ex-
tensive entries on Operation NEPTUNE.
Myron J. Smith, Jr. AIR WAR BIBLIOGRAPHY, 1939–1945:
ENGLISH LANGUAGE SOURCES. VOL. 1: THE
EUROPEAN THEATER [444].
Arthur S. White. A BIBLIOGRAPHY OF REGIMENTAL HIS-
TORIES OF THE BRITISH ARMY [515].
Janet Ziegler. WORLD WAR II: BOOKS IN ENGLISH, 1945–
1965. Stanford, Calif., 1971. [535].

ATLASES

Vincent J. Esposito. THE WEST POINT ATLAS OF AMERI-
CAN WARS. VOL. II, 1900–1953. New York, 1959.
[156]. Includes excellent maps and commentary of Allied and German movements during the Normandy campaign. The area occupied by the Allies on July 24 (D-48)
at the time of the St. Lô breakout was territory they had
hoped to have on D+5. By that date, though the Allies
had suffered some 122,000 casualties, the equivalent of
34 divisions were in Normandy. German estimates
placed their own losses at about 117,000. The Allies
very quickly made up for time lost. By D-100 they were
on the German border whereas according to their original plans, they expected at that time to be at the Seine.
John Keegan. THE TIMES ATLAS OF THE SECOND
WORLD WAR [270]. The best atlas on the war. The
maps of D-Day show the Normandy coast as seen from
the sea.
Barrie Pitt, and Frances Pitt. THE MONTH-BY-MONTH
ATLAS OF WORLD WAR II [384].
Peter Young. ATLAS OF THE SECOND WORLD WAR. New
York, 1974. [532].

BIOGRAPHICAL DICTIONARIES

John Keegan, and Catherine Bradley. WHO WAS WHO IN
WORLD WAR II [271].
David Mason. WHO'S WHO IN WORLD WAR II [328].
Provides short evaluations of key figures.
Christopher Tunney. A BIOGRAPHICAL DICTIONARY OF
WORLD WAR II [486]. Follows a narrative rather than
a critical approach so as to catch the feeling and spirit of
the war years.
Elizabeth-Anne Wheal, Stephen Pope, and James Taylor. A
DICTIONARY OF THE SECOND WORLD WAR

[513]. The volume contains entries on Normandy, NW Europe, and Caen.

ENCYCLOPEDIAS

Christopher Chant. THE ENCYCLOPEDIA OF CODE NAMES OF WORLD WAR II [92].
R. Ernest Dupuy, and Trevor N. Dupuy. THE ENCYCLOPEDIA OF MILITARY HISTORY: FROM 3500 B.C. TO THE PRESENT [139].
John Keegan. ENCYCLOPEDIA OF WORLD WAR II [266].

DOCTORAL DISSERTATIONS

Calvin Christman, and Dennis Showalter. "Doctoral Dissertations in Military Affairs" [96], continuing series published in MILITARY AFFAIRS from 1973 to 1988.
Allan R. Millett, and Franklin B. Cooling. DOCTORAL DISSERTATIONS IN MILITARY AFFAIRS: A BIBLIOGRAPHY [352].

GUIDES

John T. Bookman, and Stephen T. Powers. THE MARCH TO VICTORY: A GUIDE TO WORLD WAR II BATTLES AND BATTLEFIELDS FROM LONDON TO THE RHINE [57]. The section on Normandy is a first-rate guide to the museums, monuments, cemeteries, and sites associated with the battle.
Patrice Bousel. D-DAY BEACHES REVISITED [59]. The oldest guide to the Normandy beaches, it presumes that you have a great deal of time to spend touring Normandy.
Tonie Holt, and Valmai Holt. THE VISITOR'S GUIDE TO NORMANDY LANDING BEACHES, MEMORIALS

AND MUSEUMS [236]. The Holts are well known for conducting battlefield tours, including Normandy.

MUSEUMS

Arromanches-les-Bains: Exposition Permanente du Debarquement. From the panoramic window of this museum can be seen the remains of a Mulberry artificial harbor just off the coast.

Bayeux: Musee Memorial de la Bataille de Normandie. Houses an extensive collection of weapons, mementos, and uniforms from the different armies that fought in Normandy.

Caen: The Battle of Normandy Museum was opened in 1988 and provides a multisensory re-creation of the sights, sounds, and purpose of D-Day. The magnificent glass and stone museum, referred to as the Memorial for Peace, stands atop an ancient stone quarry. Just below the rear of the building is the entrance to what was once the headquarters bunker of the German 716th Infantry Division. The American memorial stone is made of Tennessee marble.

Portsmouth: The D-Day Museum in this city contains the OVERLORD Embroidery, 80 meters (272 feet) in length, which depicts key scenes from the Normandy campaign.

HISTORIC SITE

The famous D-Day Wall Map may be viewed by prior appointment at Southwick House, Portsmouth, England. It was from this house at 0415 hours, June 5, that General Eisenhower said, "Let's go"—the signal to begin the invasion.

HISTORIC VESSELS

H.M.S. BELFAST, which took part in the June 6 bombardment, may be toured on the Thames River near the Tower of London. The battleship TEXAS bombarded the beaches and Cherbourg. It is now preserved and displayed at the San Jacinto

Battleground and Monument outside Houston at Laporte, Texas. The destroyer LAFFEY (DD-724) also bombarded the beach during the landings. It is now on exhibit at Patriots Point, near Charleston, South Carolina. The former LST-393 carried tanks and troops ashore on D-Day. It is now named HIGHWAY 16 and is a laid-up automobile ferry at Muskegon, Michigan. The Liberty Ship JEREMIAH O'BRIEN, the last unaltered Liberty, also carried troops on D-Day. It is now a historic ship exhibit at Fort Mason, San Francisco. The U.S. Army tug MAJOR ELISHA HENSON, LT-5, is now a decommissioned Army Corps of Engineers tug, NASH, and may be a historic ship exhibit in Rochester, New York.

Chapter 3

THE SECOND FRONT

INTRODUCTION

The long-awaited cross-Channel attack on June 6, 1944, marked the end of a great Anglo-American strategic dispute over when the Second Front should be launched against Hitler's fortress Europe. The Second Front was the key issue of the middle period of the war and arguments about this question already fill libraries.

Although the United States and Britain committed themselves to a "Germany first" strategy in 1941–42, exactly what form operations against Germany should take became a matter of sharp controversy. In popular mythology, American strategy is pictured as single-mindedly devoted to a massed frontal attack on Germany, while the British are seen as Mediterranean obsessed in their strategic thinking. While the truth is much more complicated than either of these caricatures, Richard M. Leighton noted in his 1963 article "Overlord Revisited: An Interpretation of American Strategy in the European War, 1942–1944" [294], that "This notion of two divergent strategies has, in fact, become part of the American legend of World War II."

Gordon A. Harrison, CROSS-CHANNEL ATTACK [212], the official U.S. Army history published in 1951, rejected the "common misconception that the whole idea of invading northwest Europe was an American idea and an idea that the British resisted—that is simply not true." The belief that the British were against invading northwest Europe and that they had to be pushed into it, continues to have widespread currency in many accounts of World War II.

The number of primary and secondary sources on the Second Front issue is formidable. The first history of Anglo-American operations in western Europe based on first-hand experience and study of the available evidence was Chester Wilmot, THE STRUGGLE FOR EUROPE [522]. A young Australian who had served as a war correspondent, Wilmot credited Churchill with a Balkan strategy designed to prevent Russian domination of eastern Europe. After the book's publication, however, Churchill wrote to the author denying that his advocacy in 1943 of Mediterranean and Balkan operations was based on his fears of "Stalin's ambitions."

The view that British strategy was based on a tradition of maritime warfare against European powers with larger armies, and as a consequence its policy-makers had a greater appreciation of strategic flexibility is presented by John Ehrman in volume V of the official British history GRAND STRATEGY [141]. The United States with greater resources and strength preferred to follow a single, well-prepared plan. Ehrman rejected the Balkan "myth" and argued that Churchill saw the impossibility of a major Balkan campaign (unlike his friend General Smuts who did favor such an approach).

Maurice Matloff in his essay, "Wilmot Revisited: Myth and Reality in Anglo-American Strategy for the Second Front," which appeared in the 1971 Eisenhower Foundation volume D-DAY: THE NORMANDY INVASION IN RETROSPECT [146], also rejected the notion that Churchill favored a major Balkan campaign.

OPERATION SLEDGEHAMMER

At the Washington Conference (ARCADIA) between President Roosevelt and Prime Minister Churchill in December 1941, soon after Pearl Harbor, a return to the Continent seemed remote and uncertain. American planners were still in basic agreement with the British that Germany must be worn down step by step before delivering the coup de grace in the last stages of the war. Not until after ARCADIA did U.S. planners develop the concept of preparing for a single main offensive effort—the cross-Channel invasion—to avoid dispersion of effort.

By February 1942, in a memorandum written by Dwight D. Eisenhower, who was then Chief of the War Plans Division in the War Department, the Army expressed its eagerness to take early action to "draw off from the Russian front sizeable portions of the German Army." In April, George C. Marshall, U.S. Chief of Staff, and Harry Hopkins, the President's personal advisor, flew to London to obtain British support for a landing in 1942 (SLEDGEHAMMER) followed by the main invasion in 1943 (ROUNDUP). Sir Alan Brooke, Chief of the Imperial General Staff, described a midnight session as a "momentous meeting at which we accepted their proposals for offensive action in Europe in 1942 perhaps, and in 1943 for certain."

This quick British agreement surprised many, including Churchill's personal physician Sir Charles Wilson, later Lord Moran, who felt the decision was not normal behavior. Lord Moran, CHURCHILL: TAKEN FROM THE DIARIES OF LORD MORAN [362], was published in 1966. Based on extensive research in newspapers and public opinion polls is the dissertation of Dennis E. Harris, "The Diplomacy of the Second Front: America, Britain, Russia and the Normandy Invasion" [210].

Marshall and Hopkins left for home pleased with their mission's apparent success. By June, however, British leaders had concluded that any 1942 attack would end in disaster. Rather than remain idle for the remainder of the year in preparation for a 1943 crossing, they proposed an invasion of North Africa,

GYMNAST (later renamed TORCH) in place of SLEDGEHAM-
MER. Although the British expressed their continued support for
a full-scale operation in 1943, the conviction arose among Americans that British losses in World War I and defeats in World War
II had made the British reluctant to engage in any Second Front
operation.

The official British reaction to SLEDGEHAMMER can be
found in J. R. M. Butler, GRAND STRATEGY [81], Chapter
XXIV, "A Second Front? The Marshall Plan."

The failure of the Dieppe Raid on the French coast in August
1942 pointed to the pitfalls of mounting an invasion without
adequate preparations. Over 1,000 Canadians and British were
killed, and over 100 RAF planes were lost in the raid.

Michael Howard (formerly of Oxford University and now at
Yale) has contributed greatly to our understanding of British
strategy. His book THE MEDITERRANEAN STRATEGY IN
THE SECOND WORLD WAR [244] argues that Churchill's
Mediterranean strategy was less an obsession with "sideshows"
than based on a natural desire to exploit success in that theater of
operations.

An article by Hew Strachan, "The British Way in Warfare
Revisited," published in *The Historical Journal* [463], also
concludes that the British emphasis on North Africa and Italy in
1942–43, and the postponement of the Second Front to 1944, were
the result of purely practical arguments rather than based on any
traditional "British Way of Warfare."

The standard biography of Marshall is Forrest C. Pogue,
GEORGE C. MARSHALL: ORGANIZER FOR VICTORY
[386]. Pogue argues that Marshall championed the Second Front
in order to end the European War quickly, thereby releasing forces
for the Pacific. In Marshall's view, GYMNAST and later Mediterranean operations were wasteful diversions or "like throwing
snowballs into hell." Making excellent use of the American
military archives, Mark A. Stoler, THE POLITICS OF THE
SECOND FRONT: AMERICAN MILITARY PLANNING AND
DIPLOMACY IN COALITION WARFARE, 1941–1943 [462],

concludes that Marshall's thinking was as much political as military. Besides Marshall's desire to defeat Germany quickly so as to concentrate on Japan, Stoler also argues that Marshall's call for a Second Front in early 1942 was intended to counter British strategic influence as well as that of the U.S. Navy.

Following the British veto of SLEDGEHAMMER, President Roosevelt approved in July Churchill's suggestion for a landing in North Africa to tighten the ring around Germany. Roosevelt had already promised the hard-pressed Russians a Second Front in 1942 and GYMNAST would be better than simply preparing for a 1943 ROUNDUP. Roosevelt also felt that it was vital to get American public opinion involved in the European War at a time when Pearl Harbor had riveted its attention on the Pacific. The notion of a campaign in French North Africa was not Churchill's alone: Roosevelt was also interested in GYMNAST. In his memoirs, Secretary of State for War Stimson referred to the operation as "the President's great secret baby."

Roosevelt, like Churchill, was flexible about where and when Germany should be attacked. However, an essay by Brian Loring Villa, "The Atomic Bomb and the Normandy Invasion," [497] argues unconvincingly that Roosevelt was impatient for a cross-Channel attack and that he "never made a step in the direction of the atomic partnership until Churchill had moved closer toward the Normandy invasion."

General Marshall was the American champion of a Second Front in northwest Europe, and he strongly disagreed with GYMNAST. If forced to abandon SLEDGEHAMMER, Marshall proposed that the United States adopt a Pacific first strategy. Admiral King, who preferred a Pacific first approach, agreed fully with the Army Chief of Staff. Most historians have regarded Marshall's temporary advocacy of a Pacific first approach as a bluff to scare the British into agreeing to cross-Channel operations. In his article, " 'The Pacific-First' Alternative in American World War II Strategy," [461] Mark Stoler concludes that substantial evidence supports the view that the Pacific first proposals in 1942 and 1943 were "quite serious." With SLEDGEHAMMER

cancelled, increased U.S. forces were deployed to the Pacific on
the assumption that ROUNDUP was impossible in 1943. As of
July 1943, the 29th Infantry Division was still the only American
division in the United Kingdom. The United States was deploying
more troops against Japan than against Germany.

A well-written British account of the thirty-month-long invasion debate is W. G. F. Jackson, "OVERLORD": NORMANDY
1944 [254].

U.S. War Department plans for a 1942 cross-Channel attack
can be found in Maurice Matloff and Edward M. Snell, STRA-
TEGIC PLANNING FOR COALITION WARFARE, volume 1,
1941–1942 [330]. Volume 2 covers the period 1943–1944. Another invaluable official account, one much more critical of War
Department planners during the early stages of the war, is Ray S.
Cline's WASHINGTON COMMAND POST: THE OPERA-
TIONS DIVISION [99]. For the uncertain logistical outlook for
a cross-Channel operation in 1942 see Richard M. Leighton and
Robert W. Coakley, GLOBAL LOGISTICS AND STRATEGY,
1940–1943 [295]. Leighton has a chapter entitled, "Cross-Channel versus Mediterranean Attack Decisions at the Cairo-Teheran
Conferences," in Kent R. Greenfield, COMMAND DECISIONS
[196]. The former editor of "The U.S. Army in World War II"
series, Kent R. Greenfield, in his book AMERICAN STRATEGY
IN WORLD WAR II: A RECONSIDERATION [195] published
in 1963 discounted suspicions that the British were not wholehearted believers in a cross-Channel "power-drive" as soon as
conditions made its success possible, namely the dispersal of
German strength and a sufficiency of landing craft.

American military strategy is analyzed by Russell F. Weigley
in his book, THE AMERICAN WAY OF WAR: A HISTORY OF
UNITED STATES MILITARY STRATEGY AND POLICY
[505]. Weigley argues that American strategy in the twentieth
century, calling for direct confrontation with the main enemy
force, was in the tradition of U.S. Grant during the American
Civil War.

A Marshall protégé and influential strategic planner who traveled to London in April 1942 was Colonel (later General) Albert C. Wedemeyer. His views were expressed in WEDEMEYER REPORTS [503]. Wedemeyer believed that improved tactical and strategic mobility would prevent any return to a "stalemate of the trenches." Wedemeyer would later claim that he favored a Second Front in 1942 so as to block future Soviet expansion. British strategy, Wedemeyer said, was motivated primarily by imperial considerations.

Another Army planner in favor of SLEDGEHAMMER and a vociferous opponent of GYMNAST was Joseph Stilwell. Stilwell wanted to send the President a list of "65 reasons why we should not do GYMNAST." THE STILWELL PAPERS [459].

The attitude of navy planners toward SLEDGEHAMMER is referred to in Thomas B. Buell, MASTER OF SEA POWER: A BIOGRAPHY OF FLEET ADMIRAL ERNEST J. KING [77]. Among the doubters (aware perhaps of what Buell calls America's glaring inexperience in amphibious warfare in 1942) were Kelly Turner and Admiral Harold R. Stark. Fleet Admiral King, however, supported the plan. Buell says King should have known better but conjectures that he had needed Marshall's support for the Guadalcanal assault in August. Admiral King's own memoirs are important, FLEET ADMIRAL KING: A NAVAL RECORD [278]. According to Wedemeyer, in his conversations with King, the Fleet Admiral expressed his firm conviction that the British did not have any intention of crossing the Channel to invade Europe "except behind a Scotch bagpipe band." At the same time, Wedemeyer was sure that landing craft intended for a cross-Channel attack were being sent surreptitiously to the Pacific.

Both at the time of OVERLORD and later, such air force commanders as Carl Spaatz of the USAAF and Arthur Harris of British Bomber Command questioned the need for a large-scale landing in northwest Europe, believing instead that a properly conducted strategic air war would eliminate the need for a major ground campaign in the West. An extreme air force position is presented by William F. Moore, in his paper, "Overlord: The

Unnecessary Invasion," [360] argues that the German army had been beaten in the East and that the Normandy invasion was unnecessary. He concludes that Overlord was the last opportunity for the Army to play a major role in winning the European War; Marshall, he claims, "simply could not let such an opportunity pass."

An invaluable source on the thinking of American and Allied leaders at the time is Robert E. Sherwood, ROOSEVELT AND HOPKINS, AN INTIMATE HISTORY [434], based on Hopkins' personal papers and many official documents. On War Department policy, consult the Stimson memoirs, ON ACTIVE SERVICE IN PEACE AND WAR (with McGeorge Bundy) [460]. Stimson served as Secretary of State for War. Another inside view of the Second Front controversy is to be found in Admiral William D. Leahy's memoirs, I WAS THERE [289]. Leahy served as Roosevelt's Chief of Staff.

One way to become a virtual participant in the Second Front debate is to read the verbal exchanges between the Combined Chiefs of Staffs at the Allied conferences. The discussions are found in FOREIGN RELATIONS OF THE UNITED STATES: THE CONFERENCES AT WASHINGTON AND QUEBEC, 1943 [167]. Tempers could become frayed as happened at a heated afternoon session at the Cairo Conference in November 1943: "Brooke got nasty," Stilwell recorded, "and King got good and sore. King almost climbed over the table at Brooke. God, he was mad! I wish he had socked him." THE STILWELL PAPERS [459].

CHURCHILL AND THE SECOND FRONT

In the protracted and often bitter Second Front dispute, Churchill often appears as the arch-villain who unnecessarily delayed the invasion.

An essential documentary source is Warren F. Kimball, CHURCHILL AND ROOSEVELT: THE COMPLETE CORRESPONDENCE [275], which contains the messages exchanged between the two leaders. Kimball's introductory essay, "Their Relationship, Their Correspondence," is highly recommended to the reader.

Churchill's personal history of THE SECOND WORLD WAR [97] is a fundamental source. In volume V, CLOSING THE RING, Churchill is more defensive than in its predecessors. "It has become a legend in America," he complained, "that he [Churchill] strove to prevent the [OVERLORD] expedition and that he tried vainly to lure the Allies into a mass invasion in the Balkans." He rejects both accusations. He corrects Eisenhower, whose memoir CRUSADE IN EUROPE [142] had appeared in 1948, for having taken his remark "I am hardening on this operation," made three days before D-Day, as meaning that, in the past, he had been against a cross-Channel operation.

Sir Arthur Bryant's THE TURN OF THE TIDE [76], based on the diaries of General Sir Alan Brooke (later Viscount Alanbrooke) presents the strategic ideas and opinions of the quick-minded, intent, and often acerbic CIGS (Chief of the Imperial General Staff). Brooke's strategy was to wear German forces down before attempting a cross-Channel invasion. In December 1942, Churchill told Brooke that the Army would have to fight the German Army in 1943, saying, "You must not think that you can get off with your 'Sardines' (referring to Sicily and Sardinia) in 1943." Later, intoxicated by Italy's rapid collapse, Churchill became more interested in an operation towards Vienna. As D-Day approached, Brooke found Churchill "over-optimistic" as regards prospects of the cross-Channel invasion, while Brooke himself dreaded that D-Day might be "the most ghastly disaster of the war."

Martin Gilbert's magnum opus, the multivolume official biography WINSTON S. CHURCHILL (Sir Winston's son, Randolph, completed the first two volumes), chronicles the day by day, often hour by hour, actions of Churchill in his 1,417-page Volume VII, ROAD TO VICTORY, 1941–1945 [184]. Gilbert states that Churchill's preference was for a cross-Channel landing in 1943 "if only adequate forces for a successful re-entry to the

Continent could be assembled in this country." Generally speaking, Gilbert allows Churchill to speak for himself without analysis or interpretation.

An anti-Churchill assessment is Trumbull Higgins, WINSTON CHURCHILL AND THE SECOND FRONT [229], published in 1957. His thesis is that Churchill prolonged the war by his opposition to American cross-Channel proposals in 1942 and by his later advocacy of Mediterranean "adventures." Walter Scott Dunn, SECOND FRONT NOW, 1943 [137], also attacks the Mediterranean strategy.

The largest "if" concerning the Second Front controversy is whether or not a 1943 invasion of France could have ended the war sooner. The view that D-Day could have succeeded a year earlier is taken by John Grigg in his book 1943: THE VICTORY THAT NEVER WAS [197]. The Normandy campaign provides ample opportunity to play armchair strategist and "what-ifs." We do know that Hitler fought a decisive tank battle in the East in July 1943. Had those panzers been deployed in the West to meet an Allied invasion, the outcome might have been very different from the result a year later.

THE SOVIET UNION AND THE SECOND FRONT

In July 1941, following Hitler's attack on the Soviet Union, Stalin requested British fronts "somewhere in the Balkans or France, capable of drawing away from the Eastern Front thirty to forty divisions." Lord Ismay, in his MEMOIRS [253], observes that Stalin "might as well have demanded the moon." The British had just enough landing-craft to lift one brigade across the Channel. Hitler had 250 divisions, of which only 150 had advanced in the Soviet Union.

In August 1942, Churchill had the unpleasant task of informing Stalin that there would be no immediate Second Front. During the discussions with Stalin, Churchill used the famous "soft underbelly" metaphor: "it was our intention," said Churchill, "to attack the soft belly of the crocodile as we attacked his hard snout." It should be noted that Churchill did not propose substituting Mediterranean operations for the cross-Channel assault.

In the spring of 1943, the Allies appointed General Frederick E. Morgan as chief of staff to the Supreme Allied Commander (not yet named) and directed him to begin planning for the invasion of northwest Europe. However, with priority given to the Mediterranean in 1943 and the allocation of resources to the Pacific theater to permit offensives there, it became obvious that a cross-Channel assault was unlikely before 1944.

Any possibility that the Second Front might be delayed beyond 1944 ended at the Teheran Conference in November 1943 when Stalin insisted that OVERLORD be given priority.

After the Second World War, Soviet authors writing on the Second Front issue consistently reflected the dogma of the Communist Party that Anglo-American strategy was intended to have the USSR and Germany exhaust each other in a protracted war. The most important indication of Soviet thought concerning the Second Front is to be found in the six-volume HISTORY OF THE GREAT PATRIOTIC WAR OF THE SOVIET UNION, 1941–1945, published in 1960; see G. A. Deborin [125].

Colonel V. Sekistov, in his article, "Why the Second Front Was Not Opened in 1942," [433] published in the *Soviet Military Review*, claims that it is "an open secret" that the Western Allies (meaning the "ruling circles") cherished an unspoken hope that Germany and the USSR would bleed each other white. In contrast to their governments, Sekistov writes that the Second Front had the "wholehearted support" of people in the West.

V. G. Trukhanovsky, in his study of WINSTON CHURCHILL [483], writes that Churchill's strategy was designed to mask his real motive which was to block the Red Army in the Balkans and establish "reactionary regimes" in those countries.

Another Soviet historian of the Cold War era, Oleg Rzheshevsky in his OPERATION OVERLORD [418] minimizes the importance of the Normandy campaign compared to the Eastern Front. The belief is again reiterated that the West wanted to weaken the Soviet Union and use their own forces to enforce a "diktat" at the end of the war.

In May 1985, when signs appeared that the Cold War was beginning to thaw, a joint Soviet–U.S. television program was produced to commemorate the end of World War II in Europe. A group of American and Russian citizens exchanged experiences and opinions in a broadcast via satellite. The international broadcast was expanded into a book edited by Helene Keyssar and Vladimir Pozner, REMEMBERING WAR: A U.S.-SOVIET DIALOGUE [274], published in 1990.

Four decades after the end of World War II, Soviet participants in the broadcast were still critical of the fact that D-Day did not take place until June 1944. Admiral Nikolai Ivliyev relayed the story of a Soviet who had become so disillusioned about a Second Front that when asked by a British reporter, "How do you feel about D-Day," he replied, "Fuck off, all you do is promise; you never do anything!" In rebuttal to Soviet criticism, Elliott Roosevelt, the President's son, explained that even in 1944, the Normandy invasion was "nip and tuck."

Chapter 4

PLANNING FOR OVERLORD

INTRODUCTION

When President Roosevelt announced on the 1943 Christmas Eve broadcast the selection of General Dwight D. Eisenhower as Supreme Commander of the Allied Expeditionary Force that was to liberate Europe, the appointment meant that an important milestone in World War II had been passed. The last great phase of the war in the West was at hand and as Forrest C. Pogue wrote in his official study THE SUPREME COMMAND [387], "peace seemed somehow nearer than it had before."

First published in 1954 and reprinted in 1978, Pogue's study of SHAEF (Supreme Headquarters Allied Expeditionary Force) is based on both documentary sources and over a hundred interviews with the senior political and military leaders in the European war. The Pogue interviews are deposited in the U.S. Army Military History Institute at Carlisle Barracks, Pennsylvania. The "peppery" Rear Admiral George E. Creasy, who served as chief of staff to Admiral Ramsay (the Allied Naval Commander in Chief), told Pogue that "too much tripe" had been written about the beaches. Creasy doubted that the artificial harbors (MUL-

BERRIES) had justified themselves. Captain J. Hughes-Hallett, R.N., a senior OVERLORD planner, told interviewer Pogue that "Monty's talk of his original intention to hinge on Caen is absolutely balls."

To continue, however, before SHAEF there was COSSAC, and prior to COSSAC there was Combined Operations.

COMBINED OPERATIONS

The first step on the long road to D-Day began in 1940, shortly after Dunkirk, when Churchill appointed World War I naval hero Admiral Sir Roger Keyes as head of "Combined Operations" to conduct raids on Nazi-occupied Europe. Combined Operations was Britain's first joint (three-service) headquarters, and played an absolutely essential role in developing the techniques of amphibious landings. An excellent history of the Combined Operations staff, written by a former director, is Brigadier Bernard Fergusson, THE WATERY MAZE. THE STORY OF COMBINED OPERATIONS [161].

In the fall of 1941, Churchill appointed a young dynamic naval officer, Captain Lord Louis Mountbatten as head of Combined Operations. He was even given a seat on the British Chiefs of Staff Committee. Mountbatten recalled that the Prime Minister told him in "more or less these words": "You are to prepare for the invasion of Europe, for unless we can go and land and fight Hitler and beat his forces on land, we shall never win this war." During World War I, Churchill had suggested the idea of an artificial harbor, and in May, 1942, he sent a note to Mountbatten about the subject: "They *must* float up and down on the tide. . . . Don't argue the matter. The difficulties will argue for themselves." Mountbatten's contributions to OVERLORD are presented in Philip Ziegler's first-rate biography MOUNTBATTEN [536]. A fleet of specialized landing craft was a prerequisite of a successful invasion. A wide range of landing craft was needed for a variety of precise ends, each manned by specially trained crewmen. A new science and new industry were called for, and in the spring of 1942, both were in their infancy.

On the question of where a cross-Channel invasion should take place, primarily a choice between either the Pas de Calais (directly across the Channel from Dover) or Normandy (still within range of air cover), Mountbatten came down strongly in favor of Normandy. "Thank God," he declared, "I won through and we landed successfully in Normandy." More objectively, his biographer concludes that to attribute the decision exclusively to Mountbatten "would be over-generous."

COSSAC

At the Casablanca Conference in January 1943, the Allies agreed that while Mediterranean operations should be given priority in order to exploit their success in North Africa, preparations for a cross-Channel invasion should continue. It was still too early to appoint a Supreme Commander, as this would need a man of established reputation, but they did agree to the appointment of Lieutenant General Frederick E. Morgan as Chief of Staff to the Supreme Commander (Designate). His task was to begin preliminary planning for the Allied invasion of northwest Europe. The old code name ROUNDUP was discarded and replaced by the code name Operation OVERLORD, selected by Churchill. The name given to the new organization was taken from the first letters of Morgan's new title and became known simply as COSSAC with its headquarters in Norfolk House, St. James's Square, London.

Operation OVERLORD

The story of COSSAC, the forerunner of SHAEF, is described by General Frederick E. Morgan in his account, OVERTURE TO OVERLORD [363]. A bulky package of papers containing everything that had been done to date about the cross-Channel invasion was handed to Morgan. Morgan himself records that the

actual beginning of Operation OVERLORD began with a conference code named RATTLE chaired by Mountbatten who had
suggested that the planners leave London and examine every
aspect of the invasion issue at Largs, in Scotland, where there
was a Combined Operations training school. By the end of the
Conference, Morgan records that there was enthusiasm that a
cross-Channel invasion could succeed. These events are also
discussed in a Thirtieth Anniversary volume, D-DAY [489]
published in 1974 by Warren Tute (a naval officer who had been
actively involved in Combined Operations), John Costello, and
Terry Hughes.

By the end of July, Morgan and his Anglo-American staff had
produced a 113-page plan for Operation OVERLORD that proposed where and how the invasion should be launched: a three-
division assault in the Caen sector of Normandy. Interestingly, in
light of what happened later, the report noted that "much of it
[the terrain inland] is unfavorable for counter-attack by panzer
divisions." The COSSAC planners were far more concerned at
this stage about securing an Allied bridgehead from panzer
counterattack than they were about how the terrain might hinder
an Allied breakout.

Morgan's plan was approved by the British and at the Quebec
Conference in 1943 President Roosevelt and the U.S. Chiefs also
gave their approval. The target date for the invasion of northwest
Europe was set for May 1, 1944.

The role of the Free French Central Bureau of Information and
Action in the planning of OVERLORD is described by a partici-
pant, E. Combaux, in the article "Le BCRA et l' Operation
Overlord," DEFENSE NATIONAL [105].

Ingersoll

The COSSAC plan is savagely criticized by Ralph Ingersoll in
his book, TOP SECRET [251], which was published in 1946.
Ingersoll's polemic may be considered the first "revisionist"
history of the post–World War II era since it emphasizes Allied

differences. A controversial journalist before Pearl Harbor, Ingersoll served on General Omar Bradley's staff during the war. Ingersoll ridiculed COSSAC's meticulous requirements concerning the weather, and the tide and moon conditions that the planners said needed to exist for the operation to succeed. "These jokers aside," Ingersoll regarded the conditions mentioned in the plan as being nothing more than "escape clauses" to justify the British not carrying out the operation. The difficulties facing OVER-LORD, claimed Ingersoll, were intentionally magnified and overrated by the British so as to discourage the whole idea of invasion.

Ingersoll's book created more anger on both sides of the Atlantic than any single account of the war. Ingersoll had his supporters. Bruce Catton wrote to Ingersoll that TOP SECRET was one of the most important books he had read. Ingersoll died in 1985. Roy Hoopes, a free-lance journalist who was granted personal interviews with Ingersoll, completed his book, RALPH INGERSOLL, A BIOGRAPHY [238], shortly before his subject's death.

EISENHOWER TAKES COMMAND

British Chief of the Imperial General Staff Alan Brooke and American Chief of Staff George Marshall both at one point had been regarded as the likely commander of an Allied invasion of France. Brooke's name faded as American military strength increased, and Marshall seemed certain to lead the climactic assault on Germany across the Channel. But a decision had still not been made at the time of the Teheran Conference in November 1943 where Stalin forced the issue by wanting to know who would command the OVERLORD invasion. Roosevelt could not put the decision off any longer.

Marshall's unselfishness and patriotism shone forth when Roosevelt asked him what he wanted to do and Marshall replied that he would do whatever the President felt was in the best interests of the country. Roosevelt replied, "Well, I didn't feel I could sleep at ease if you were out of Washington." Marshall, experiencing the greatest disappointment in his career, would remain as Chief of Staff, the only man who could carry the burden of that position. Informing Stalin, Marshall wrote: "The immediate appointment of General Eisenhower to Command OVERLORD has been decided on" and handed the message to Roosevelt to sign. Afterwards, Marshall sent the original to the new Supreme Commander with the note, "Dear Eisenhower: I thought you might like to have this as a memento." The article by John G. Fowler, Jr., "Command Decision" in *Military Review* [170], presents the reasons why Marshall remained in Washington.

The Eisenhower Side

The "real Eisenhower" is to be found in THE PAPERS OF DWIGHT DAVID EISENHOWER [91] edited by Alfred D. Chandler, Jr., and Stephen E. Ambrose. Published in 1970 by Johns Hopkins University, five volumes cover the war years. The volumes are superbly cross-referenced, annotated and indexed. The series includes the bulk of his correspondence and many classified papers. THE EISENHOWER PAPERS dispel the notion that Eisenhower was simply a chairman of the board or merely a coordinator.

A few months after publication of the Eisenhower papers, Stephen E. Ambrose, who had served as associate editor of the Johns Hopkins project, published his impressive, THE SUPREME COMMANDER: THE WAR YEARS OF GENERAL DWIGHT D. EISENHOWER [12]. Just as lively is Ambrose's study, EISENHOWER [6] published in 1983. Rather than comparing Eisenhower's role during the Normandy campaign to that of a football coach, which was the analogy drawn by Eisenhower's wartime chief of staff, Walter Bedell Smith, in his book, EISENHOWER'S SIX GREAT DECISIONS: EUROPE, 1944–1945 [449], Ambrose considered Eisenhower more a cheerleader than a coach. Another comparison might be made with that of a symphony conductor.

Eisenhower's chauffeur and confidante, Kay Summersby, wrote her memoir, EISENHOWER WAS MY BOSS [468], soon after the war. In 1976 there appeared PAST FORGETTING: MY LOVE AFFAIR WITH DWIGHT D. EISENHOWER [469]. The Ambrose biography contains a plausible explanation of that relationship.

On the question of Eisenhower's ability as a military commander, the Ambrose article, "Eisenhower's Generalship" in PARAMETERS [7], argues that while Eisenhower was "excessively cautious" in the Mediterranean theater, in northwest Europe he showed "boldness and a willingness to take risks." Also useful is Merle Miller, IKE THE SOLDIER: AS THEY KNEW HIM [351].

Piers Brendon, IKE: HIS LIFE AND TIMES [65] writes that Eisenhower was the best qualified person in the world to command what was probably the most complex military operation in history. No one else, he observes, could match Eisenhower's experience of mounting amphibious operations. Other favorable assessments of Eisenhower are Martin Blumenson and James L. Stokesbury, MASTERS OF THE ART OF COMMAND [52], and E. K. G. Sixsmith, EISENHOWER AS MILITARY COMMANDER [440].

Besides the military experience that he gained in the Mediterranean, Eisenhower demonstrated enormous ability to get people of different nationalities and viewpoints (not to mention prima donnas) to work together. He insisted that his staff officers lay aside their national differences which led some U.S. officers to complain that "Ike is the best commander the British have."

The Normandy campaign required a degree of unity and cooperation between different nations, armed services and peoples than ever before in history. Suspicion, distrust, and mutual dislike had often marked the Anglo-American relationship. No one did more to promote a spirit of teamwork than Eisenhower.

Eisenhower's own modest, deeply moving memoir, CRUSADE IN EUROPE [142], appeared in 1948 to popular acclaim. Historian Edward Mead Earle praised the book as perhaps the best by a soldier-historian since Caesar's Commentaries. Eisenhower tried to please everybody in the book, but there were still some who felt slighted. In an interview with U.S. *News and World Report* [147], Eisenhower answered some of the critics. In the same interview he made the surprising remark, "An amphibious landing is not a particularly difficult thing."

It must be kept in mind that in the early years of the Cold War with Soviet power an only too real menace, there was a strong desire not "rehash" Anglo-American wartime disputes such as occurred during the Normandy campaign. For this reason, military historian Carlo D'Este has described CRUSADE IN EUROPE as providing an "intentionally bland version" of events.

The importance of personal relations in the British-American partnership is covered in John Eisenhower's (Eisenhower's son) ALLIES: PEARL HARBOR TO D-DAY [144]. His thesis is that in large part military matters are intensely personal and political. David Eisenhower has written a 1,000-page book covering the wartime experience of his grandfather.

At Eisenhower's direction, his naval aide, Captain Harry C. Butcher kept a diary of day-to-day happenings at SHAEF. Although Butcher was a firsthand witness to great events, his account MY THREE YEARS WITH EISENHOWER: THE PERSONAL DIARY OF CAPTAIN HARRY C. BUTCHER [80], contains some revealing raw material but for the most part is disappointing. The work is heavy on trivia and chitchat. Eisenhower claimed that he disliked the book. Butcher's approach, however, may be gathered from what he told Mamie Eisenhower in 1945: he was "compiling a second Bible and creating a second Jesus." The book did in fact much to enhance Eisenhower's popularity.

The memoir of General Omar Bradley, A SOLDIER'S STORY [63], offered his personal perspective on the Normandy campaign. Far less reliable as a primary source is Bradley's, A GENERAL'S LIFE [64], published in 1983. Completed mainly after Bradley's death in 1981 by Clay Blair, the account is a posthumous "ghost" autobiography.

Memoirs of Eisenhower's staff at SHAEF include Kenneth Strong, INTELLIGENCE AT THE TOP: THE RECOLLEC-

TIONS OF A BRITISH INTELLIGENCE OFFICER [465] and
E. J. Kingston McCloughry, THE DIRECTION OF WAR [279],
which contains perceptive characterizations of the SHAEF com-
manders. A valuable bibliographic monograph is Robert D.
Bohanan, DWIGHT D. EISENHOWER: A SELECTED BIBLI-
OGRAPHY OF PERIODICAL AND DISSERTATION LITER-
ATURE [55], that may be obtained from the Eisenhower Library
in Abilene, Kansas.

Eisenhower's official report to the Combined Chiefs of Staff
on the Normandy campaign, as well as the entire war in northwest
Europe is the REPORT BY THE SUPREME COMMANDER
TO THE COMBINED CHIEFS OF STAFF ON THE OPERA-
TIONS IN EUROPE OF THE ALLIED EXPEDITIONARY
FORCE, 6 JUNE 1944 TO 8 MAY 1945 [143].

The Other Side

One of the most unflattering characterizations of Eisenhower
is presented in Ingersoll's book TOP SECRET [251]. He labeled
Eisenhower a pawn of the British, a front-office stooge, a
yes-man. "General Eisenhower," wrote Ingersoll, "of course,
had nothing whatever to do with leading the invasion." The
selection of Eisenhower was part of the British master plan,
alleged Ingersoll, to put a pliable American in charge of the whole
Overlord operation so that the British could command the land,
sea, and air forces. In a letter to Montgomery, Eisenhower called
Ingersoll's account a "trashy book."

In the Alanbrooke diaries, THE TURN OF THE TIDE and
TRIUMPH IN THE WEST [76] edited by Arthur Bryant and
published between 1957 and 1959, the wartime Chief of the
British Imperial General Staff described Eisenhower as "Just a
co-ordinator, a good mixer, a champion of inter-Allied co-oper-
ation . . . no real commander." In his own memoir, CRUSADE
IN EUROPE [142], Eisenhower had described Brooke as merely
adroit and shrewd.

Montgomery

Eisenhower's CRUSADE IN EUROPE [142] included vignettes of Eisenhower's contemporaries, one of whom was Field Marshal Bernard Law Montgomery. Montgomery commanded Allied ground forces during the Normandy campaign. Eisenhower assumed direct command of field operations on September 1, 1944. Montgomery's official account ("ghosted" by David Belchem, one of Montgomery's senior staff officers) appeared in 1947, entitled, NORTH TO THE BALTIC [359]. For the first time in print, the Montgomery interpretation of what had happened in Normandy was laid before the public, namely that the battle of Normandy had gone exactly according to plan: by which he meant that it had always been his plan to draw the panzer divisions to the British front while Bradley broke out on the American flank.

Carlo D'Este, in his important book, DECISION IN NORMANDY [128], published in 1983, demonstrates that Montgomery's original intentions were *offensive*; only after the failure to take Caen did Montgomery's strategy change to one of deliberately drawing panzer divisions onto the British front. Until D'Este's account, the controversy over Montgomery's "master plan" would divide not only the Normandy campaign participants themselves, but historians who tended to line up on one side or the other in the dispute.

Montgomery's refusal to admit that he ever made such a change in his battle plan, together with both honest mistakes and his own prima donna personality, both then and later resulted in considerable Montgomery-bashing.

By coincidence, Montgomery's account appeared almost simultaneously as Francis de Guingand's book (Montgomery's chief of staff), OPERATION VICTORY [198]. Taking issue with Ralph Ingersoll and other critics of Montgomery, Freddie de Guingand ably defended his chief without overlooking his faults. Eisenhower, Bradley, and Bedell Smith all praised de Guingand's book (perhaps in part because he agreed with Eisenhower's later broad-front strategy for defeating Germany). Reviewer Forrest Pogue judged the book a fair-minded account.

LOGISTICS

General Studies

From artillery and bulldozers to dental chairs and ambulances, providing logistical support for the Normandy campaign was immense. The U.S. Army official history on the subject is Roland G. Ruppenthal, LOGISTICAL SUPPORT OF THE ARMIES, VOL. I [415]. An important series of articles by Frank A. Osmanski, "The Logistical Planning of Operation Overlord," [378] appeared in *Military Review*. A bird's eye view of the planning for the Normandy invasion, with emphasis on the work of the Royal Army Service Corps, is described by John Dalgleish in his book, WE PLANNED THE SECOND FRONT [120]. The Canadian side is told by Arnold Warren in his work, WAIT FOR THE WAGON: THE STORY OF THE ROYAL CANADIAN ARMY SERVICE CORPS [500]. Other useful accounts are Albert Norman's, OPERATION OVERLORD, DESIGN AND REALITY: THE ALLIED INVASION OF WESTERN EUROPE [373], and Hawthorne Daniel's, FOR WANT OF A NAIL: THE INFLUENCE OF LOGISTICS ON WAR [121], which is an excellent introduction to the subject of logistics.

Critics of Logistical Planning

A harsh critic of SHAEF logisticians, who he says were not cast in the heroic mold, is Martin van Creveld. In SUPPLYING WAR: LOGISTICS FROM WALLENSTEIN TO PATTON [494], van Creveld faults what he calls "the excessive conservativism and even pusillanimity that characterized the logistic planning for Overlord from beginning to end." A paper by former logistics planner Harold L. Mack, THE CRITICAL ERROR OF WORLD WAR II [318], presents an eyewitness and critical view of the conduct of the Normandy campaign from the perspective of a logistics planner.

Mulberries

The two MULBERRIES or artificial harbors that were built and then towed across the Channel to the invasion beaches have been the subject of many books, including: Guy Hartcup, CODE NAME MULBERRY: THE PLANNING, BUILDING AND OPERATION OF THE NORMANDY HARBOURS [214]; L. C. Brownlowe, THE MULBERRY PROJECT [75]; Edward Ellsberg, THE FAR SHORE [151]; Harold Hickling, SAILOR AT SEA [227]. Vice Admiral Hickling had charge of the planning and operation of the "Mulberry" project.

The continuous and spectacular part played by U.S. Seabees in assembling and constructing the Rhino Ferries and causeways is described by John J. Manning in his article, "Normandy's Artificial Harbors,"[322] published in *The Military Engineer*. Other literature bearing on the subject includes Walter Karig, "Rhinos and Mulberries," [264] in *United States Naval Institute Proceedings*; Alfred Stanford, FORCE MULBERRY: THE PLANNING AND INSTALLATION OF THE ARTIFICIAL HARBOR OFF U.S. NORMANDY BEACHES IN WORLD WAR II [458]; U.S. Army Corps of Engineers, Special Brigade Group, OPERATION REPORT NEPTUNE, OMAHA BEACH [490]. Chapter 13 of the report is entitled, "Construction of the Harbor."

Special Studies

On a less well known but nonetheless important aspect of the invasion, the delivery of mail to the troops, there is on the British side the monograph by K. S. Holmes OPERATION OVERLORD . . . HISTORY OF THE WORK OF THE ARMY POSTAL SERVICES IN RELATION TO OVERLORD [235].

A superficial treatment of a neglected subject, camouflage, is Seymour Reit's, MASQUERADE: THE AMAZING CAMOU-

FLAGE DECEPTIONS OF WORLD WAR II [399]. The author describes how both sides disguised landmarks, war materials, factories, and other important targets. A more general treatment is Guy Hartcup, CAMOUFLAGE: A HISTORY OF CONCEAL-MENT AND DECEPTION IN WAR [213].

THE PRESS

"Appendix A" ("SHAEF and the Press") in Forrest Pogue, THE SUPREME COMMAND [387] is a brief summary of SHAEF's efforts to keep the public informed about the Invasion without compromising the security of operations. Needless to say, there were difficulties encountered in trying to reconcile these opposing interests.

On June 6, 1944, 461 reporters were signed up at SHAEF to cover D-Day. Of that number, however, only twenty-seven American reporters actually went ashore with the first wave of forces. Ernie Pyle declared that practically every newspaper in the U.S. had sent a reporter except *The Dog World*. The numbers pale in comparison to those covering Operation DESERT STORM in 1991: nearly 1,400 reporters were in Saudi Arabia when the ground war began. Relations between the military and the press are sensibly discussed in an article by Richard Halloran, "Soldiers and Scribblers Revisited: Working with the Media," which appeared in *Parameters* [204].

Ernie Pyle, who was America's favorite war correspondent in World War II, wrote about his Normandy experiences in the book, BRAVE MEN [394]. Like many others, Pyle dreaded the cross-Channel invasion, expecting U-boat, E-boat, and aircraft attack— "Yet nothing whatever happened." He arrived on Omaha Beach the morning after D-Day—"a pure miracle that we ever took the beach at all." He provides a realistic view of the fighting in the Normandy hedgerows. A useful index is provided with the names and home towns of the soldiers that he met in action. Also useful is David Nicholas's ERNIE'S WAR: THE BEST OF ERNIE PYLE'S WORLD WAR II DISPATCHES [371].

Charles C. Wertenbaker's INVASION [510] provides a reporter's description of the D-Day invasion to the occupation of Cherbourg. The book is illustrated with photos taken by Robert Capa of *Life* magazine.

Correspondent for the London *Daily Mail*, Noel Monks, wrote his account of D-Day in EYE-WITNESS [357].

Comments regarding the press can be found in Lewis H. Brereton, THE BRERETON DIARIES [66]. He commanded the U.S. Ninth Air Force during the Normandy campaign.

A. J. Liebling, a wartime journalist for *The New Yorker*, captures the atmosphere of the period in his book, NORMANDY REVISITED [304]. He described his experience aboard a U.S. Coast Guard LCI on D-Day in an article, "Cross-Channel Trip," *New Yorker* [303].

A comparison between official campaign accounts and civilian press reports is the subject of an M.A. thesis by Bickford E. Sawyer, Jr., "The Normandy Campaign from Military and Press Sources" [423].

Radio reports describing the Normandy campaign can be found in the Columbia Broadcasting System, FROM D-DAY THROUGH VICTORY IN EUROPE: THE EYEWITNESS STORY AS TOLD BY WAR CORRESPONDENTS ON THE AIR [104]; Desmond Hawkins, WAR REPORT: A RECORD OF DISPATCHES BROADCAST BY THE BBC'S WAR CORRE-SPONDENTS WITH THE ALLIED EXPEDITIONARY FORCE, 6 JUNE 1944–5 MAY 1945 [220]; the National Broad-casting Company, THIS IS THE STORY OF THE LIBERATION OF EUROPE FROM THE FALL OF ROME TO VICTORY AS NBC NEWSMEN RELAYED IT BY RADIO TO AMERICAN LISTENERS [367].

MEN AND WOMEN IN THE ARMED SERVICES

The important contribution of American women is described by Mattie E. Treadwell in the official history, THE U.S. ARMY IN WORLD WAR II, SPECIAL STUDIES: THE WOMEN'S

ARMY CORPS [482]. There is a fine study by historian Lee B. Kennett entitled, G.I.: THE AMERICAN SOLDIER IN WORLD WAR II [273]. An oral history of the rank-and-file U.S. soldier is found in Edwin Palmer Hoyt's book, THE GI'S WAR: THE STORY OF AMERICAN SOLDIERS IN EUROPE IN WORLD WAR II [246]. The contribution made by Black American soldiers is the subject of Bernard C. Nalty's book, STRENGTH FOR THE FIGHT. A HISTORY OF BLACK AMERICANS IN THE MILITARY [366]. For the experience of Black GIs in Britain see Graham Smith, WHEN JIM CROW MET JOHN BULL. BLACK AMERICAN SOLDIERS IN WORLD WAR II BRITAIN [443]. The official U.S. Army study, published in 1966, was written by Ulysses Lee, THE EMPLOYMENT OF NEGRO TROOPS [291].

Although English professor Paul Fussell's deep sense of personal disillusionment with World War II colors some of his conclusions concerning the meaning of the war, his book WARTIME: UNDERSTANDING AND BEHAVIOR IN THE SECOND WORLD WAR [175] is stimulating and offers some fresh insights into human behavior during the Normandy campaign.

Chapter 5

AIR AND NAVAL PREPARATIONS

INTRODUCTION

For the Normandy invasion, the Allies massed 5,000 ships—landing craft and midget submarines to battleships. American air strength alone was 13,000 aircraft, including 4,500 bombers. It was the largest, most complex military operation in history. In early May 1944, the date had been set for June 5, but by the night of June 3—after a glorious May—the weather had turned stormy and the invasion had to be postponed one day. Though the weather remained chancy, the monumental operation could not be held off longer.

THE TRANSPORTATION PLAN

Before the Allies could invade Normandy, the German Air Force had to be knocked out, at least to the point where it could not endanger the invasion. Beginning in June 1943, almost simultaneously with COSSAC planning, U.S. and British bombers launched operation POINTBLANK with the objective of destroying the enemy's military and industrial complex. Between

January and June, 1944, the five months before D-Day, the Luftwaffe suffered tremendous losses. Although not directly related to the needs of OVERLORD, the Combined Anglo-American bomber offensive had acted as a magnet that drew up hundreds of German fighters to be destroyed by Thunderbolts and Mustangs. To a large degree, the Strategic Bombing Campaign had been a kind of "Second Front."

By the early months of 1944, however, the question of how the heavy bombers could give full support to the upcoming invasion became a bone of bitter contention. The actual air forces designated in direct support of OVERLORD were under the command of Air Chief Marshal Trafford Leigh-Mallory. The 9th U.S. Air Force and the British 2nd Tactical Air Force made up what was called the Allied Expeditionary Air Forces or the AEAF. American and British heavy bombers were not under his command.

In March 1944, Leigh-Mallory put forward the AEAF railway bombing plan, variously known as "the Transportation Plan," "the Zuckerman Plan," "the Tedder Plan" and so forth. Based on an analysis by Professor Solly Zuckerman, scientific advisor to AEAF, the proposal called for the bombing of railway marshalling yards in Belgium and France in order to prevent German reinforcements from reaching Normandy. The plan required the use of the Allied heavy bombing forces. U.S. and British bomber commanders strongly resisted the plan, since they did not wish to relinquish control over their bombers or be diverted from the strategic bombing offensive against Germany.

Official Histories and Autobiographies

For the U.S. Air Force account of the railways bombing plan, see Wesley Frank Craven and James Lea Cate, THE ARMY AIR FORCES IN WORLD WAR II, VOL. III, EUROPE: ARGUMENT TO V-E DAY, JANUARY 1944 TO MAY 1945 [112]. In his foreword to the 1983 reprint (the original account was published in 1951), Richard H. Kohn, former chief U.S. Air Force historian, reminds the reader that "Like all history, The Army

Air Forces in World War II reflects the era when it was conceived, researched, and written. " On the subject of the overall interdiction program during the Normandy campaign, the editors claim that it was "spectacularly successful. "

The official British counterpart is Sir Charles Webster and Noble Frankland, THE STRATEGIC AIR OFFENSIVE AGAINST GERMANY 1939–1945, VOL. III: VICTORY. PART 5 [501]. The authors clearly prefer Sir Arthur Tedder, who was Deputy Supreme Commander of SHAEF, over Sir Arthur Harris, the Commander in Chief of British Bomber Command. Tedder pushed the Transportation Plan. Shortly after his appointment as Deputy Supreme Commander, a German intelligence assessment of Tedder reported: "Obviously we are dealing here with one of the most eminent personalities amongst the invasion leaders." Tedder's autobiography, WITH PREJUDICE. THE WAR MEMOIRS OF MARSHAL OF THE ROYAL AIR FORCE LORD TEDDER [473], is essential reading. The author admits in the introduction, "Frankly, I am completely prejudiced." A British Army view of Tedder can be found in W. G. F. Jackson, "OVERLORD": NORMANDY 1944 [254].

Zuckerman and the Bomber Chiefs

The struggle for the adoption of the Transportation Plan is described in fascinating, if prejudiced, detail by the Plan's author, Solly Zuckerman, in one of the best autobiographies to come out of World War II. Zuckerman's FROM APES TO WARLORDS [538] is the story of a poor Jewish boy from South Africa who rose to a position where he could observe policy-making at the highest level. A prewar zoologist, Zuckerman became an expert in bomb damage assessment. His plan proposed a bomber offensive against the railway network of northwest Europe in place of the inadequate original AEAF plan which had called for only two weeks of strategic bombing before D-Day.

The commander of U.S. Strategic Air Forces in Europe, Carl "Tooey" Spaatz, opposed the plan, as did Arthur "Bomber"

Harris of Bomber Command. Long before and long after D-Day, Spaatz contended that a properly conducted strategic air war (centered on oil) would eliminate the need for a ground invasion, or at least reduce it to a mere occupational operation. For Spaatz's perspective thirty years later, see Carl A. Spaatz and Ira C. Eaker, "Reflections on Overlord," [454] in *Air Force Magazine*.

For a pro-Spaatz, strategic bombing point of view, see Haywood S. Hansell, Jr., THE AIR PLAN THAT DEFEATED HITLER [207]. Harris felt just as strongly as Spaatz that the Transportation Plan was a mistaken diversion of the bomber offensive although he downplayed his opposition to the plan in his memoir, BOMBER OFFENSIVE [209].

The bomber chiefs made life especially difficult for SHAEF air commander Leigh-Mallory. The story is told in E. J. Kingston McCloughry, THE DIRECTION OF WAR [279]. The author writes that Leigh-Mallory and his staff received little recognition of their contribution to the Normandy campaign whereas the Army was rewarded generously in the honors list. While on his way to join Mountbatten as Air Commander in Chief S.E. Asia, Leigh-Mallory and his wife were killed in a plane crash in the early fall of 1944.

Eisenhower adopted the Transportation Plan since he said it was only necessary to show that there would be *some* reduction, however small, in the enemy's ability to reinforce his troops in Normandy. When Churchill had nagging thoughts about how many French civilians might be killed in the program, and expressed his concern to Roosevelt, the President came down strongly in support of Eisenhower's decision.

In his autobiography, Zuckerman had mentioned by name "an intensely serious and hostile young man" who at the time had opposed the railway bombing plan. The young man was Charles P. Kindleberger and in 1944 he belonged to a small group of American economists called the "Enemy Objectives Unit" (EOU) in the Economic Warfare Division of the American Embassy. Another member of the group was Walt W. Rostow. Kindleberger discusses his objections to Zuckerman's bombing plan in his article, "Zuckerman's Bomb: World War II Strategy," [277] that appeared in *Encounter*. Kindleberger, who advocated bombing bridges instead of marshalling yards, wrote that Zuckerman had possessed "an overblown reputation." The argument continued in that journal, see Lord Zuckerman replies, "Bombs and Illusions in World War II" [539], and Charles P. Kindleberger, "A Rejoinder" [276].

The position of the "bridge advocates," including information on how many tons of explosives were required to destroy a bridge, can be found in Walt W. Rostow, PRE-INVASION BOMBING STRATEGY: GENERAL EISENHOWER'S DECISION OF MARCH 25, 1944 [408].

The OVERLORD air dispute is the subject of an essay by Herman S. Wolk, "Prelude to D-Day: The Bomber Offensive," *Air Force Magazine* [529]. The article favors the bombing ideas of Spaatz.

The power struggle, wrangling, and heated meetings between strategic air forces, SHAEF, Americans, British, and individual personalities is described in Carlo D'Este, DECISION IN NOR-MANDY [128].

The reminiscence of a member of a bomber crew is found in Stewart Menaul, "Reflections on D-Day 1944," published in *Contemporary Review* [340]. After facing the anti-aircraft fire over Germany, the sorties over northern France flown in support of the Transportation Plan saw a dramatic drop in casualties.

The Transportation Plan went ahead. Spaatz and Harris did their best to support OVERLORD. In the three months of bombing before D-Day, the 8th Air Force and Bomber Command conducted more than twenty thousand sorties and dropped 65,000 tons of bombs on eighty targets. Two bombs were dropped outside of the Normandy area for every bomb dropped in the assault area so as not to arouse German suspicions. Montgomery had asked that Normandy be sealed off to a depth of 150 miles. German reinforcements did reach the battle zone, but usually only after serious delays. The 9th and 10th SS Panzer Divisions traveled 1,300 miles by train from Poland to Metz without too much difficulty. But it took them as long to make the 200 miles from Metz to the front as to come from the East.

THE TACTICAL AIR FORCES

Providing direct support for the Allied ground troops during the Normandy campaign were the tactical air forces. General Lewis H. Brereton commanded the U.S. Ninth Air Force and Air Marshal Sir Arthur Coningham the British 2nd Tactical Air Force. "Mary" Coningham (a New Zealander, his nickname was derived from Maori) and Montgomery were scarcely on speaking terms during the Normandy campaign. The ambitious Coningham had felt slighted by Montgomery after the North African campaign.

9th U.S. Air Force and 2nd British TAF

THE BRERETON DIARIES [66] are an important and highly readable first-hand account of the events, personalities, and controversies of that spring and summer of 1944. An idea of the work that went into planning for the invasion may be grasped from the extent of the Ninth Air Force's plan for operation NEPTUNE alone: 847,500 words covering 1,376 pages; 4½ inches thick, the plan weighed 10 pounds 3 ounces.

On the eve of D-Day, Eisenhower had told paratroopers, "If you see a plane overhead, it'll be ours." Fewer than fifty enemy planes were seen in the battle area all day. In the first twenty-four hours of D-Day, the combined Allied air forces flew more than 13,000 sorties. Praising the close air support given American forces on Omaha Beach, General Elwood "Pete" Quesada, who commanded the IX Tactical Air Command of the Ninth Air Force, declared that "History may show they saved the day." See Kenn C. Rust, THE 9TH AIR FORCE IN WORLD WAR II [414]. William R. Dunn flew with the 406th Fighter Group on D-Day. His activities are described in his book, FIGHTER PILOT: THE FIRST AMERICAN ACE OF WORLD WAR II [138]. Dunn witnessed the incredible sight of the Allied invasion from 16,000 feet over the Channel. Although living in a tent camp on a primitive airfield in Normandy was unglamorous, he mentions aircraft belly tanks filled with beer and the potency of a keg of calvados—the local Normandy beverage.

British 2nd TAF operations are covered by Christopher F. Shores in his book 2ND TAF [436]. Although the Luftwaffe put in hardly any appearance on D-Day, Shores rejects what he terms "the oft-repeated legend" that the Luftwaffe had been driven from the skies, and never posed any serious threat. This was "far from being true," he writes, and once German reinforcements were pushed through to the Normandy front, RAF units experienced a level of combat not seen over Europe since 1940, other than the Dieppe Raid in 1942.

Sir Basil Embry, MISSION COMPLETED [152], describes the operations of No. 2 Group, 2nd TAF. Embry commanded the unit which consisted of British, French, Dutch, and Polish squadrons. He discusses the effectiveness of German flak.

An excellent book on the air operations preceding and supporting the invasion is Humphrey Wynn and Susan Young, PRELUDE TO OVERLORD [530]. The book provides the names of all the squadrons and wings involved in OVERLORD, their airfield location, and type of planes. Some personal exploits of Coastal Command pilots against U-boats are presented in Michael Wilson and A. S. L. Robinson, COASTAL COMMAND LEADS THE INVASION [523].

Scale models of northern France and the landing areas, together with seven million photographic prints, were produced every month at Medmenham, England, before the Normandy invasion. This important story is told by Andrew J. Brookes in his book, PHOTO RECONNAISSANCE [68].

The effectiveness of Allied power during the Normandy campaign is the subject of Richard P. Hallion's book, STRIKE FROM THE SKY: THE HISTORY OF BATTLEFIELD AIR ATTACK, 1911–1945 [203]. Hallion writes that the decisiveness of air power in Normandy is "beyond question." The same author's article, "Battlefield Air Support: A Retrospective Assessment," that appeared in

Airpower Journal [202], cites the Normandy campaign as an example of where interdiction predominated over close air support.

All was now ready for D-Day, and during the early days of June all Allied aircraft were painted with black and white identification bands around the fuselages and wings, in an effort to try to avoid Allied aircraft from being fired on by "friendly" anti-aircraft guns. For D-Day, AEAF disposed the full strength of 2nd TAF and 9th Air Force.

OPERATION NEPTUNE

Operation NEPTUNE, the naval and amphibious phase of OVERLORD, was commanded by Admiral Bertram H. Ramsay who had retired shortly before the war after forty-two years in the Royal Navy. Recalled to duty in 1939, Ramsay organized the naval forces for the Dunkirk evacuation. Later he helped plan TORCH, commanded a task force in the Sicilian invasion, and became British naval commander in the Mediterranean. He was appointed Allied Naval Commander in Chief, Expeditionary Force, in the fall of 1943, and served in that post until his death in a plane crash in 1945. Ramsay had the ability to make quick decisions, an unruffled personality, and a unique knowledge of combined operations; most importantly, he possessed a happy gift for cooperation. Admiral Kirk, the senior American naval officer in OVERLORD, did not like Ramsay, whom he criticized for laying down the NEPTUNE plans in too much detail.

As Myron J. Smith, Jr., has commented in his bibliography WORLD WAR II AT SEA [447], the naval contribution to the cross-Channel invasion of 1944, though large and important, has often been skimmed over. After many rehearsals and mock landings, the timing for the Invasion rendezvous was so perfect that ships sailing from as far away as Northern Ireland arrived on schedule. Failure might well have made Dieppe look like a picnic.

With D-Day delayed from May until June in order to obtain another month's production of the critically important landing craft, Churchill swore about the necessity of waiting for "some god damned things called LSTs. " For an account of these vessels, see Paul Lund and Harry Ludlum, THE WAR OF THE LANDING CRAFT [313].

Besides transporting and supplying the Invasion forces, the Navy's role included providing gunfire support. The chief of staff of the U.S. 1st Infantry Division, after reflecting on the hard-fought battle on Omaha Beach, wrote, "I am now firmly convinced that our supporting naval fire got us in; that without that gunfire we positively could not have crossed the beaches." Not only was naval gunfire critical during the landings at the water's edge but it continued to give aid as the ground forces advanced inland for several days.

With the U.S. Navy heavily committed to the Pacific War, the Royal Navy assumed most of the responsibility for NEPTUNE. The 2,700 vessels of the attack force, including landing craft, were divided into the Western Naval Task Force (destined for Omaha and Utah beaches) under Rear Admiral Alan G. Kirk, USN, and the Eastern Naval Task Force (destined for Sword, Juno, and Gold beaches) under Rear Admiral Sir Philip Vian, RN (see Admiral Philip Vian, RN, ACTION THIS DAY: A WAR MEMOIR [496]). These were further subdivided into task forces responsible for each of the five landing beaches. Admiral John L. Hall, Jr., commanded the amphibious landings at Omaha Beach. A eulogistic biography of Hall is Susan H. Godson's, VIKING OF ASSAULT: ADMIRAL JOHN LESLIE HALL, JR., AND AMPHIBIOUS WARFARE [187]. This was the first biography to be written about one of the specialists of amphibious warfare in the ETO (European Theater of Operations). Rear Admiral D. P. Moon commanded Force U ("Utah Beach"). Ramsay considered Moon "a fine type of U.S. officer. Efficient and alert."

Admiral Ramsay's original dispatch was printed under the title, REPORT BY ALLIED NAVAL COMMANDER-IN-CHIEF EXPEDITIONARY FORCE ON OPERATION NEPTUNE [395].

General British and Canadian Accounts

Published in 1946, the story of Lieutenant Commander Kenneth Edwards, RN, OPERATION NEPTUNE [140], remains an important first-hand account of the naval side of the Invasion. The vast scope of the naval activities, at least in part, is covered in a short book by Vice Admiral Brian Schofield, OPERATION NEPTUNE: SEA BATTLES IN CLOSE-UP SERIES [429]. The official British history of World War II was written by Captain Stephen W. Roskill. The Normandy campaign is to be found in THE WAR AT SEA, 1939–1945 VOL. III, PART II [406]. Roskill, who died in 1982, completed the last volume of his official history in 1961.

Military historian Correlli Barnett, while not an official naval historian, has proven a worthy successor to Roskill with his recent book, ENGAGE THE ENEMY MORE CLOSELY: THE ROYAL NAVY IN THE SECOND WORLD WAR [27]. Making good use of sources that have become available over the past thirty years, Barnett presents a particularly striking account of naval planning for the Normandy Invasion. Barnett sees the cross-Channel invasion as the culmination of British naval achievement.

The Canadian Navy's part in the Normandy landings is described in Joseph Schull, THE FAR DISTANT SHIPS: AN OFFICIAL ACCOUNT OF CANADIAN NAVAL OPERATIONS IN THE SECOND WORLD WAR [431].

General American Accounts

Samuel Eliot Morison authored the massive fifteen volume official history of American naval operations in World War II. Volume XI, THE INVASION OF FRANCE AND GERMANY, 1944–1945 [365], describes the U.S. Navy's contribution to the assault and includes graphic descriptions of destroyers firing from almost point-blank range in support of the assault troops on D-Day. Morison rejects the charge that Admiral King starved the cross-Channel attack to feed the Pacific. About 124,000 U.S. naval personnel participated directly or indirectly in the invasion. Although the Royal Navy supplied "the lion's share" of ships for gunfire support, 2,493 U.S. Navy ships and craft were assembled for Operation NEPTUNE.

Fleet Admiral Ernest J. King's attention was divided between the Marianas and OVERLORD. Saipan and Normandy—two mammoth amphibious assaults a half world apart. Personalities are discussed by Thomas B. Buell, MASTER OF SEA POWER: A BIOGRAPHY OF FLEET ADMIRAL ERNEST J. KING [77].

The French Navy

The actions of the French Navy are described by Paul Auphan and Jacques Mordal in their book, THE FRENCH NAVY IN WORLD WAR II [19]. Besides smaller ships, two French cruisers, *Georges-Leygues* and *Montcalm*, commanded by Admiral Robert Jaujard, participated in the invasion. The French naval contingent was attached to Rear Admiral Kirk's U.S. Naval Force. The old French battleship *Courbet* was scuttled offshore in order to serve as a breakwater for the artificial port of Arromanches.

Correspondents at Sea

The landing and gunfire support is described by Desmond Tighe, "Report of the Reuter Correspondent for the Combined Allied Press Aboard a British Destroyer," in Louis L. Snyder, MASTERPIECES OF WAR REPORTING [450]. The actions of USS *McCook* in support of Omaha Beach are told by Martin Sommers, "The Longest Hour in History: The U.S. Destroyer *McCook* in the Normandy Invasion," *Saturday Evening Post* [452]. Also by the same correspondent, "Right Hard Rudder! All Hands Below!": The U.S. Battleship *Texas* in the Bombardment of Cherbourg," *Saturday Evening Post* [453].

Minesweeping, Frogmen, and U-Boats

In early June 1944, one hundred and fifty British, Canadian, American, French, and other Allied minesweepers began the dangerous task of clearing passages for the invasion convoys. Minesweeping operations are discussed in William H. Pugsley,

"First the Mine Sweepers," in John Winton, THE WAR AT SEA: THE BRITISH NAVY IN WORLD WAR II [526], and Richard Fisher, WITH THE FRENCH MINESWEEPERS [163]. The dangerous task of removing explosive devices from the beaches before the landings is the subject of Edward T. Higgins, WEBFOOTED WARRIORS: THE STORY OF A "FROGMAN" IN THE NAVY DURING WORLD WAR II [228]. The critical battle to prevent Admiral Doenitz's U-boat fleet from interfering with the invasion is discussed by Alfred Price in AIRCRAFT VERSUS SUBMARINE: THE EVOLUTION OF THE ANTI-SUBMARINE AIRCRAFT, 1912 TO 1972 [389]. A 20,000-square-mile area, far greater than any previously attempted, had to be intensively patrolled by day and by night, so that a U-boat on the surface in that area would be seen on radar at least once every thirty minutes. Air patrols had to be maintained for an indefinite period, twenty-four hours a day. Fortunately, by the beginning of June 1944, only nine of the forty-nine U-boats allocated to the counter-invasion task carried the new schnorkel breathing device. Many of the conversion kits were in their packing cases, trapped in goods yards by the Allied air bombardment of the French railway system. If a U-boat did manage to penetrate the air patrol screen, it still had to run the gauntlet of some three hundred Allied warships. On June 7, one Canadian Liberator sank two U-boats in less than thirty minutes. By June 12, Admiral Theodor Krancke, the commander of Naval Forces West, was forced to admit defeat. He ordered all submarines without the schnorkel to return to their bases.

German oyster mines, either acoustic or magnetic, dropped from long-range GAF bombers emerged as the most effective weapon of the German Air Force. By June 21, forty-four Allied ships had been sunk or damaged by mines. During July and August, the number of Allied ships sunk or damaged by mines averaged four per week.

Karl Doenitz, the commander of the German Navy, transcribed his diaries while in prison after the war, see his MEMOIRS: TEN YEARS AND TWENTY DAYS [132]. Friedrich Ruge,

Rommel's naval advisor who after the war became head of the German Federal Republic's navy, wrote a general history entitled, DER ZEEKRIEG: THE GERMAN NAVY'S STORY, 1939–1945 [410]. Another survey is Hellmuth Dahms, DER ZWEITE WELTKRIEG [119].

Chapter 6

OPERATION FORTITUDE

INTRODUCTION

To cross the English Channel in force and confront the German army, which could be reinforced from anywhere in Europe, even from the Russian front, promised to be the most dangerous military undertaking in history. The deception or cover plan, codenamed FORTITUDE, entailed execution of a massive intelligence campaign to deceive Germany about the date and place of the Invasion. An entire fake army—the non-existent First U.S. Army Group of thirty divisions—was created simply to convince the enemy that the main landing would be in the Pas de Calais area under Patton. Next to ULTRA, it was the most carefully kept secret of the European war. General Omar Bradley called FORTITUDE "the biggest hoax of the war."

OPERATION FORTITUDE

Not until four decades after the war was the veil that covered the vital realm of deception and intelligence gradually removed. British use of German agents in Britain was known in outline from

Sir John Masterman's DOUBLE-CROSS SYSTEM [329]. Then, in the mid-1970s, the entire veil was dropped as the extent of British intelligence activities during World War II became known to the public. The secret after-action history of the Normandy deception operation, originally completed in 1949, appeared in 1979, and is known as the Hesketh Report, see Colonel Roger Hesketh, "FORTITUDE": A HISTORY OF STRATEGIC DE-CEPTION IN NORTH WESTERN EUROPE, APRIL 1943 TO MAY 1945 [225].

In another disclosure of the 1970s, R. V. Jones in his important memoir, MOST SECRET WAR [259], wrote about the tremendous effort to neutralize German radar before D-Day. On the night before D-Day, Lancaster bombers dropping "Window" (strips of metal foil) created "spoof" convoys headed for landings in northern France—but not Normandy. Of the forty-seven German radar stations operating three weeks before D-Day, hardly more than half a dozen were able to transmit on the vital night. Jamming measures during the crossing of the Channel reduced this figure even more. While Allied planes suffered heavy losses from the anti-aircraft guns defending the radar stations, another element in the enemy's ability to detect the invasion had been neutralized.

After 1975, under the thirty-year rule, the British government began releasing volumes of secret intelligence documents through the Public Record Office at Kew. Charles Cruickshank, an experienced historian, after working in the once highly secret intelligence files, published his interesting and important book, DECEPTION IN WORLD WAR II [115]. He covers the main deception schemes, above all, the effort to build up in Hitler's mind the idea that there was a large U.S. army in Kent under Patton which was going to land where the German general staff expected the Allies to land, on the beaches south of Calais. FORTITUDE was expected to operate not only before the invasion, but for several weeks after D-Day. Cruickshank's later book, STRATEGIC AND OPERATIONAL DECEPTION IN THE SECOND WORLD WAR [116], contains a chapter by T. L. Cubbage entitled, "The Success of Operation FORTITUDE:

Hesketh's History of Strategic Deception." The operation to build dummy LSTs, called "Bigbobs," to fool the Germans is covered in Peter Tooley, OPERATION QUICKSILVER [481]. John Mendelsohn collected relevant documents in the U.S. National Archives on Operation FORTITUDE, see his book, COVERT WARFARE: BASIC DECEPTION AND THE NORMANDY INVASION [341].

Also useful is the account by Jock Haswell, D-DAY: INTELLIGENCE AND DECEPTION [218]. Like OVERLORD itself, he notes, the deception operation designed to shield it was the largest of its kind ever attempted in the history of warfare. The author also discusses the presence of the German 352nd Infantry Division behind Omaha Beach. The fire of its two forward regiments gave the beach its nickname of Bloody Omaha. He claims that because a third regiment had been sent to search for paratroopers that did not exist (operation TITANIC had involved dropping hundreds of dummy paratroopers), the 352nd could not counterattack on Omaha Beach.

The only U.S. Army Air Force officer involved in the planning and execution of FORTITUDE, Captain (later Major) H. Wentworth Eldredge, tells his story in "Biggest Hoax of the War," in *Air Power History* [148]. Stephen Ambrose points to the importance of Intelligence in, "Eisenhower, the Intelligence Community, and the D-Day Invasion," *Wisconsin Magazine of History* [8]. His article, "The Secrets of Overlord," in *The Quarterly Journal of Military History* [11], explains the Double-Cross operation which involved turning German spies in the United Kingdom. The British sprung the trap on D-Day, using the double agents to send the Abwehr, German Intelligence, false information concerning the whereabouts of the real cross-Channel invasion.

A large and immensely detailed account of German Intelligence is David Kahn's, HITLER'S SPIES: GERMAN MILITARY INTELLIGENCE IN WORLD WAR II [262]. Kahn finds that German Intelligence activities were very poor.

HINSLEY

The publication in 1988 of the massive concluding part of the official history of British intelligence in World War II, F. H. Hinsley, BRITISH INTELLIGENCE IN THE SECOND WORLD WAR: ITS INFLUENCE ON STRATEGY AND OPERATIONS [233], debunks many of the more exaggerated accounts of clandestine episodes and covert events: the celebrated penetration by the Germans of the security of the British Embassy in Turkey, the "Cicero" case, which others have alleged, compromised operation OVERLORD, is dismissed by Hinsley as a false alarm.

Again, the wilder claims made for the total success of FORTITUDE in allegedly immobilizing the entire German 15th Army in the Pas de Calais, while the Allies established themselves in Normandy, are rejected. Hinsley is anxious to avoid attributing sole or decisive responsibility for enemy troop movements to Allied deception. He notes that the frequently cited message from the British-run double-agent "Garbo," arrived in Berlin on the evening of June 9 at the same time another agent, "Josephine," in Stockholm, sent a message warning of the danger of another assault on the Pas de Calais. The German high command recalled the 1st Panzer Division from its march on Normandy.

FORTITUDE would have failed if the Germans had had reasonably good intelligence. Instead, Germany in the weeks before D-Day lacked any source of reliable information. All German agents in the United Kingdom were controlled by the British. And not more than thirty-two overland reconnaissance flights by the GAF were recorded in daytime in the first six months of 1944. The excellence of Allied security precautions in keeping the Normandy invasion site a secret cannot be overlooked.

While based on a thorough reading of relevant British intelligence archives, open and closed, the volume has been criticized for its refusal to name names. Only Alan Turing of the cryptanalysts appears in person. Turing, mathematical genius, codebreaker, and homosexual, is the subject of a stageplay, "Breaking the Code," by Hugh Whitemore.

Sir Harry Hinsley omitted names and personalities in order to be fair and not favor one individual more than another! Military historian Nigel Hamilton has noted that the author might have conducted interviews with surviving Intelligence officers who might have helped our understanding of the way intelligence was used by commanders in the field.

ULTRA

Of all the new information that came to light in the 1970s regarding the inner history of World War II, the most astounding to the public was revelation of the ULTRA secret. At the innocuous-sounding Government Code and Cipher School at Bletchley Park, fifty miles from London, up to ten thousand persons were engaged in "breaking the code," deciphering top-secret German radio traffic. Not a word was breathed about ULTRA for thirty years, an astounding feat of collective security-mindedness.

The most celebrated of the ULTRA exposes was Frederick Winterbotham, THE ULTRA SECRET [525]. Based on memory, the book is superficial and unreliable. In that same category is Anthony Cave Brown, BODYGUARD OF LIES [71].

Making use of the ULTRA intercepts that were opened to the public at the PRO in Kew was the important book by Ralph Bennett, "ULTRA" IN THE WEST: THE NORMANDY CAM-PAIGN [38]. Bennett spent the war working at Bletchley, and he later became a Medieval historian at Cambridge. The book is complex and detailed. Two important articles by Bennett are "Ultra and Some Command Decisions," *Journal of Contemporary History* [39], and "Fortitude, Ultra and the 'Need to Know,' " *Intelligence and National Security* [37]. Bennett says that ULTRA played no part in the greatest command decision in the West—the choice of time and place for the invasion. Its chief value before D-Day was confined to revealing the dispositions the German army intended to make in an emergency. Once ashore, ULTRA gave the Allies valuable information. Bennett argues that General Omar Bradley's "momentous decision of 8 August" to drive eastward would seem to be based on information from ULTRA. He concludes, "This was surely the supreme moment of Ultra in the west, for it was responsible for a stroke upon which we can now see that the triumphant progress of the next few weeks largely depended."

Bennett strongly leans toward the view that fundamental strategic principles, such as the fact that invasion convoys could be guaranteed the greatest protection if they took the shortest sea crossing, were more important than agents' reports and Hitler's intuition in explaining German actions. He raises the important question, "How soon did SHAEF know how much of Fortitude's purpose was being achieved, and what use was made of the knowledge?"

ULTRA did not "win" the war, wrote Adolph G. Rosengarten, Jr., in his article, "With ULTRA from Omaha Beach to Weimar," *Military Affairs* [405]. The author served on a Special Liaison Unit that relayed ULTRA information to the field commanders. Rosengarten believes that ULTRA was *"primus inter pares*, some of the time but not all of the time."

Another vital source of information for the Normandy campaign were the MAGIC intercepts from the Japanese embassy in Berlin. MAGIC was the cover name for American decoding of Japanese radio communications. The Japanese ambassador, Oshima Hiroshi (a career army officer), began sending by radio on November 9, 1943, a series of messages to Tokyo in which he described in detail German defenses along the Atlantic Wall. The U.S. Army Signal Intelligence Service (SIS) at Arlington Hall Station, Virginia, intercepted and translated Oshima's virtual blueprint of Hitler's Atlantic Wall. This fascinating story is examined in the fifth of a series of articles on these secret intercepts by Carl Boyd in his article; "Significance of MAGIC and the Japanese Ambassador to Berlin: (V) News of Hitler's Defense Preparations for Allied Invasion of Western Europe,"

Intelligence and National Security [62]. Finally, there were the "astonishing" messages from Oshima indicating Hitler's belief that the decisive blow would be struck in the area of the Straits of Dover. There, in Hitler's own words, Germany would "wage an action like that of Cannae long ago." These decrypts were rushed to British Military Intelligence. OVERLORD must have seemed more feasible to Churchill, even though the margins remained very tight, remarks Professor Boyd. And small wonder that a grateful Eisenhower, soon after his return to the United States in 1945, visited Arlington Hall Station to thank personally the translators and cryptanalysts who provided his campaign in Europe with vital information about the enemy.

The world of clandestine secret agents and sabotage is covered in M. R. D. Foot, SOE IN FRANCE: AN ACCOUNT OF THE WORK OF THE BRITISH SPECIAL OPERATIONS EXECU- TIVE IN FRANCE, 1940–1944 [166]. Despite the volume being an official history, Stephen Ambrose called Foot's account better than a James Bond thriller. SOE's biggest success, writes Foot, was its help for OVERLORD. French resistance forces, acting with SOE's weapons and under SOE's general direction, pro- duced more than a thousand railway cuts in France in a week. Nearly all the main telephone cables in France were out of action on D-Day or just after it. SHAEF estimated that the actions of the French Resistance and SOE delayed by an average of two days the arrival of all German units attempting to get to Normandy. But the author's comparison with Bomber Command is tenden- tious. SOE's sabotage exploits were probably far more produc- tive, he argues, than Bomber Command's "wholesale devastation of his [Germany's] cities."

The role of the French resistance in the Normandy campaign is described by Edward G. Sollers in his article, "The Twilight War: Resistance in France, 1940–1944," *Strategy & Tactics* [451]. Sollers writes that the weeks after D-Day were the "finest moments of the French Resistance." French Marquis activities are also described in Robert B. Asprey's WAR IN THE SHAD- OWS [17], H. R. Kedward's RESISTANCE IN VICHY

FRANCE [265], and David Schoenbrun's SOLDIERS OF THE NIGHT [428]. Two helpful bibliographies are Myron J. Smith, Jr., THE SECRET WARS: A GUIDE TO THE SOURCES IN ENGLISH [445], and Roger A. Beaumont, SPECIAL OPERATIONS AND ELITE UNITS, 1939-1988: A RESEARCH GUIDE [31]. DESTINATION D-DAY [129], a 1984 video tape production of BBC Television, is an interesting presentation of the deception schemes even if more recent studies, such as those by Hinsley and Bennett, have modified earlier claims concerning FORTI-TUDE. The narration is provided by Sir Hew Wheldon who went in with the British 6th Airborne Division on D-Day.

SLAPTON SANDS

Six weeks before the Normandy invasion, the U.S. Army staged a practice landing on the Devon coast of England. In the early morning hours of April 28, nine German torpedo boats attacked, sinking two of the LSTs. Of the total 749 dead and missing, 198 were sailors and 551 soldiers. Losses were heavier than those suffered by Force U (Utah) during the actual invasion. Allied commanders were not only concerned about the loss of life and the two LSTs, but also about the possibility that the Germans might have taken any survivors prisoner, in which case the upcoming invasion would be seriously compromised. In the event, all of the officers who had been involved in the planning and knew the assigned beaches were drowned.

But forty years later, rumor, misunderstanding and media gullibility combined to create the myth that the disaster had been covered up by the authorities. A television station in Washington, D.C. ran a three-part series on the so-called cover-up. The prolific popular historian, Edwin P. Hoyt, has written a straightforward account, THE INVASION BEFORE NORMANDY: THE SE-CRET BATTLE OF SLAPTON SANDS [247]. Another account is Nigel Lewis, CHANNEL FIRING: THE TRAGEDY OF EXERCISE TIGER [297]. The best place to start is with an excellent article by Charles B. MacDonald, "Slapton Sands: The 'Cover-Up' That Never Was," that appeared in *Army* magazine [317].

Chapter 7

D-DAY, JUNE 6, 1944

INTRODUCTION

Two years of planning and preparation led up to D-Day. After weighing all the possibilities, the fifty miles of coast in Normandy, from the Vire estuary on the west to the Orne River in the east, was selected as the assault area for the Allies. Although somewhat further from English ports than the Pas de Calais, along the narrowest part of the Channel, Normandy was not as heavily fortified. The critical factor, besides the initial landing, would be the Allies' ability to reinforce and supply the assault rapidly enough both to meet the expected German counterattack and to prepare for a larger Allied offensive beyond the landing area. Could D-Day have ended in disaster for the Allies? On the twentieth anniversary of D-Day, military historian Martin Blumenson asked that very question; his answer was a strong "yes," see his article, "D-Day in Retrospect: Could the Germans Have Won?" *Army* [49]. The recent near-disasters at Salerno and Anzio in Italy were vivid reminders of the dangers that lay ahead.

Eisenhower had wisely rejected an earlier proposal by Marshall for a deep airborne drop south of Evreux, pointing out to the U.S.

Chief of Staff that the Germans had shown time and again that they did not particularly fear the threat of envelopment. Arnold, commanding general of the U.S. Army Air Forces, lamented the fact to Marshall that they had failed to convince Eisenhower that massed airborne forces could succeed in a long-range tactical role. The result of such an airborne gamble can well be imagined given what happened later at Arnhem.

On the eve of D-Day, American and British relations with Free French leader, General Charles de Gaulle, experienced one last complication when he refused to read a statement prepared by SHAEF for broadcast to the French people. The scene for what Forrest Pogue described as "a comic opera prelude to the invasion" had been set earlier. President Roosevelt refused to recognize General de Gaulle as leader of a Provisional French government until the French people had an opportunity to make a free choice. Furthermore, security for OVERLORD was so tight that the Free French government in London could not be given advance information about Allied moves, which naturally annoyed them. When de Gaulle arrived in London on June 4 from his headquarters in Algiers, the scene was set for a crisis: he refused to use the prepared speech on the grounds that it stressed too strongly French obedience to the Allied command and made no mention of the Provisional French government of which he claimed to be the leader. He also issued a last-minute ban on the embarkation of the 170 French liaison officers who were to assist the Allied forces.

When Winston Churchill heard the inaccurate report that General de Gaulle refused to broadcast, he threatened to send "this obstructionist saboteur" back to Algiers "if necessary in chains." De Gaulle rose to the occasion, however, and his broadcast to the French people went out over the BBC at six o'clock on D-Day evening. The speech had not been submitted to SHAEF in advance.

By June 1944 the number of American troops in Britain had risen to 1,526,965. The stockpile for the invasion—over and above basic loads and equipment—was 2,500,000 tons. The popular expression of the time was that only the barrage balloons kept the British Isles from sinking under the weight of men and equipment. The quiet countryside of England resembled a little bit of America with Yanks everywhere. American officers were billeted in more than forty English country homes, GIs lived in 1,200 camps, big 2½-ton trucks, jeeps, and American staff cars monopolized the narrow English roads. Pubs overflowed with troops from all Allied nations. The British accepted the Allied "invasion" in good spirits. American soldiers generously shared their candy and gum with British children.

St. Paul's School, London

On May 15, there took place at St. Paul's School in Hammersmith the great dress rehearsal for OVERLORD with the entire Allied high command present for the historic meeting before D-Day. George VI, Smuts, Churchill, Eisenhower, Montgomery, Tedder, Ramsay, Leigh-Mallory, Brooke, Bradley, Dempsey, Patton, Hodges, Simpson, Crerar, and a host of other military commanders were in attendance. The doors were shut promptly at nine A.M. Arriving late, Patton hammered on the door. After twice hammering, the doors were opened and in marched Patton.

Eisenhower's quiet confidence removed any lingering doubts about the success of OVERLORD, as did Montgomery who outlined the ground assault. Wearing battledress, Montgomery emphasized the need for aggressive and bold action to push armored thrusts deep inland, and quickly on D-Day. As we shall see, Montgomery's strategy during the Normandy campaign, and what exactly he originally intended to do, became an issue of bitter controversy that brought forth a library of books. While not underestimating his adversary Rommel, Montgomery predicted at the St. Paul's gathering that the land battle would be "a terrific party."

The Weather

Finally, everything depended on the weather. The most momentous decision of Eisenhower's life depended on the forecast of his chief meteorologist, J. M. Stagg, who recounted the episode in his memoir, FORECAST FOR OVERLORD [457]. The decision took place at Southwick House, the naval headquarters just outside of Portsmouth. The room and D-Day Wall Map can still be seen. On Sunday, June 4, with a storm imminent, the Supreme Commander postponed D-Day for twenty-four hours. Small wonder that he was smoking four packs of Camels a day. An interesting account of this period by Allan A. Michie is THE INVASION OF EUROPE, THE STORY BEHIND D-DAY [348]. Michie was a correspondent who covered Eisenhower's temporary headquarters at Portsmouth during these momentous days.

On Sunday night, with a break in the weather expected, Eisenhower gave the go-ahead. The last meeting occurred at 4:15 A.M. on Monday, June 5, to confirm or cancel the Invasion. After discussion, Eisenhower said, "O.K. We'll go."

Once on his own, Eisenhower drafted a press communiqué assuming full responsibility for the failure of OVERLORD. He put the note in his wallet and forgot about it until later. Today, the note can be seen in the Eisenhower Library, Abilene, Kansas.

GERMAN PREPARATIONS

Before 1942, victory had seemed so certain to Hitler that coastal fortifications were regarded as unnecessary. Once he was engaged in a two-front war, however, Hitler demanded an impregnable Atlantic Wall, a Fortress Europa. By the end of 1943, although the Wall was far from finished, the fortifications had become a menacing reality.

Two well-written books that describe Hitler's coastal fortifications are Alan F. Wilt, THE ATLANTIC WALL: HITLER'S

DEFENSES IN THE WEST, 1941–1944 [524], and Colin Partridge, HITLER'S ATLANTIC WALL [380].

Field Marshal von Rundstedt, who commanded all German forces in the West, dismissed the Atlantic Wall as "just a bit of cheap bluff." Gunther Blumentritt, von Rundstedt's chief of staff, wrote a biography of his former commander entitled, VON RUNDSTEDT. THE SOLDIER AND THE MAN [53]. Von Rundstedt's operations officer, Bodo Zimmerman, wrote "France, 1944," in Seymour Freidin and William Richardson's THE FATAL DECISIONS [172]. British military writer B. H. Liddell Hart conducted interviews with the German generals following the war; their views are expressed in THE GERMAN GENERALS TALK [300]. German reaction to the Teheran Conference and their confidence in being able to defeat an Allied invasion of France can be found in Louis P. Lochner, THE GOEBBELS DIARIES, 1942–1943 [306]. Nevertheless, Adolf Hitler sent Field Marshal Erwin Rommel to inspect the coastal fortifications.

Rommel and Differences over Strategy

Cornelius Ryan, in his book, THE LONGEST DAY [417], focuses on Rommel during the pre-invasion period. Rommel described the Atlantic Wall as a "figment of Hitler's cloud-cuckoo-land."

With the task of strengthening the Atlantic defenses, Rommel was appointed commander of Army Group B by Hitler. Von Rundstedt remained as Commander in Chief, West. The fragmented and muddled command structure within the German army was a major flaw. Rommel's panzer reserves were under the operational control of Hitler's OKW (Armed Forces High Command, Berlin). After the war, Von Rundstedt would plead that his authority as Commander in Chief, West, only extended as far as changing the guard in front of his gate!

A fundamental disagreement also existed among the German generals over how the panzer divisions should be deployed against an Allied invasion. Rommel's attitude toward Allied air power and its influence on his tactics is explained in his papers which were edited by B. H. Liddell Hart, THE ROMMEL PAPERS [301]. The Desert Fox had experienced Allied air power firsthand in Africa, and as a consequence he believed the panzers would have to defeat the Allies on the beaches. If the panzers were held back, Allied air power would prevent them from reaching the decisive battle. Von Rundstedt and General Geyr von Schweppenburg (commander of Panzer Group West), however, favored waiting until the Allies were ashore before committing the panzers to a decisive counterattack.

Rommel's chief of staff, Hans Speidel, wrote his memoirs, INVASION 1944: ROMMEL AND THE NORMANDY CAMPAIGN [455]. There are many minor errors of fact as he gropes through his memories searching for the reasons for defeat. Rommel's naval advisor, Admiral Friedrich Ruge, wrote the chapter entitled, "The Normandy Invasion," in the book by H. A. Jacobsen and J. Rohwer, DECISIVE BATTLES OF WORLD WAR II: THE GERMAN VIEW" [255]. There is also Ruge's own book, ROMMEL IN NORMANDY [412]. Historian Samuel W. Mitcham, Jr., is the author of a brief study, ROMMEL'S LAST BATTLE: THE DESERT FOX AND THE NORMANDY CAMPAIGN [355]. Mitcham is biased in favor of Rommel.

The German perspective is also presented by Paul Carell in his book, INVASION—THEY'RE COMING! THE GERMAN ACCOUNT OF THE ALLIED LANDINGS AND THE 80 DAYS' BATTLE FOR FRANCE [83].

From inside the OKW, there is Walter Warlimont, INSIDE HITLER'S HEADQUARTERS [498]. The oft-condemned failure of OKW to release its panzer reserve until the afternoon of D-Day is defended by Warlimont on the grounds that not until 10:30 A.M. did the HQ of Army Group B consider the situation serious enough to inform their commander, Rommel, who was in Germany attending his wife's birthday.

Rommel had also intended to visit Hitler to try to persuade him to release the panzer reserve to his control. May had passed with no invasion, when the weather had been perfect. He also reasoned, as did Hitler and the High Command, that the invasion would wait until the Russian summer offensive in late June or July.

Following the war, many of the German commanders who fought in Normandy wrote down their experiences at the request of the U.S. Army; the recollections are found in WORLD WAR II MILITARY STUDIES [130] edited by D. S. Detweiler and others. The battles of Normandy as experienced by German troops is the subject of a book by James Lucas and James Barker, THE BATTLE OF NORMANDY: THE FALAISE GAP [309]. A more general study is that by Matthew Cooper, THE GERMAN ARMY, 1939-1945 [108].

D-DAY, JUNE 6, 1944

Cornelius Ryan

In the few short months before the invasion, Rommel's ruthless drive changed the whole picture along the Atlantic Wall. Steel obstacles on the beaches, millions of mines, pillboxes, concrete bunkers, all kinds of defensive obstacles were ordered by Rommel the perfectionist to be placed along the coast. "Believe me," Rommel said to an aide, "the first twenty-four hours of the invasion will be decisive . . . for the Allies, as well as Germany, it will be the longest day." This and other unforgettable quotations—"How stupid of me, how stupid of me," was Rommel's only comment on learning that he had missed the most important battle of his life—are to be found in the old popular standard, THE LONGEST DAY: JUNE 6, 1944 [417] by Cornelius Ryan. At the time of the book's publication in 1959, on the fifteenth anniversary of D-Day, THE LONGEST DAY belonged to a comparatively new category of literature—retrospective popular journalism. The book is a good example of that genre. Ryan, a Dublin-born war correspondent who flew over the beaches on June 6, left the disputes and interpretation to others, and he

succeeded in making the reader feel and see some of the confu-
sion, fear, and courage that went into that day. Historian A. J. P.
Taylor considered Ryan's book the best in the "I was There"
category. He was not on the beaches but he created the sensation
he was. The Hollywood epic, THE LONGEST DAY, that came
to the screen in 1964 and is based on the book, was a great success.

General D-Day Accounts

Published the same year as THE LONGEST DAY were two
books by British authors: D-DAY, THE SIXTH OF JUNE, 1944
by David Howarth [245], and INVASION 1944: THE FIRST
FULL STORY OF D-DAY IN NORMANDY by John Frayn
Turner [488]. Howarth was there on D-Day. More selective in his
interviews than Ryan, his personal accounts have more depth and
literary quality. Howarth captures the heroic grandeur of the
Invasion. There is no mention of those who would rather have
stayed at home on D-Day. Turner argues that British tactics were
to avoid frontal assaults on strong points.

Walter Millis's THE LAST PHASE: THE ALLIED VICTORY
IN WESTERN EUROPE [354], published in 1946, was intended
primarily to be translated into German for the "re-education" of
the German people. Millis makes frequent mention of German
divisions, corps, and armies. Other accounts include The Army
Times, D-DAY: THE GREATEST INVASION [15] and American
Heritage, D-DAY, THE INVASION OF EUROPE [14].

For young readers, there is Milton Dank, D-DAY [122], which
is a good starting point with an excellent list of books for further
reading; Al Hine, D-DAY: THE INVASION OF EUROPE [232],
was part of the American Heritage Junior Library; Albert Marrin,
OVERLORD: D-DAY AND THE INVASION OF EUROPE
[323], published in 1982, is a lively read and concentrates on the
soldier's life and living conditions.

THE BRIDGEHEAD

The British Airborne Landings

A few minutes past midnight on June 6, Major John Howard and his glider-borne troops, elements of the 6th British Airborne Division, seized "Pegasus" Bridge over the Caen Canal to secure the vital left flank of the invasion. A vivid description of the assault is provided by Stephen E. Ambrose, PEGASUS BRIDGE, JUNE 6, 1944 [10]. The author interviewed British, German, and French survivors of the battle. An article by Wilfred P. Deac, "Vanguard of Invasion,"[124] in *British Heritage*, very briefly describes the assault. The Red Berets, who had fought D-Day's first battle, held out for thirteen hours until relieved by Lord Lovat's commandos led by a bagpiper blaring out "Blue Bonnets over the Border." The dramatic episode is recounted by Lord Lovat in his memoir, MARCH PAST [308]. Former commando leader, Peter Young, wrote STORM FROM THE SEA [534]. A new edition of Young's class memoir was published by the U.S. Naval Institute Press in 1989.

The gallant action of No. 4 Commando during the Invasion is told in Murdoch C. McDougall, SWIFTLY THEY STRUCK: THE STORY OF NO. 4 COMMANDO [333]. French forces were attached to the unit.

The commander of the 6th Airborne Division wrote his account of operations, General Sir Richard Gale, WITH THE 6TH AIRBORNE DIVISION IN NORMANDY [179], and his later memoir, CALL TO ARMS. AN AUTOBIOGRAPHY [178]. Other excellent accounts are Napier Crookendon, DROPZONE NORMANDY: THE STORY OF THE BRITISH AND AMERICAN AIRBORNE ASSAULT, D-DAY 1944 [114], and Maurice Tugwell, AIRBORNE TO BATTLE: A HISTORY OF AIRBORNE WARFARE, 1918–1971 [485].

The 9th Battalion, the Parachute Regiment, commanded by Terence Otway, was given a "Grade A stinker of a job!" To put out of action the guns of the heavily defended Merville Battery

flanking the northern beaches. That episode is retold by John
Golley in his book, THE BIG DROP: THE GUNS OF MER-
VILLE, JUNE 1944 [189].

The American Airborne Landings and Ranger Assault

On the eve of D-Day, Eisenhower had visited the 101st Airborne,
known as the "Screaming Eagles," at Newbury. In one of the most
famous photographs of World War II, 1st Lt. Gordon Stroebel, Co.
E, 502nd Parachute Infantry Regiment, is the tall soldier with the
blackened face that Eisenhower is speaking to. Stroebel recalled,
at the age of sixty-eight, that they "were pretty feisty, because they
wanted to fight." The remarks are reported by William H.
McMichael, "Journey to Victory," *Soldiers* magazine [337]. The
101st were to be harassed by clouds and anti-aircraft fire, and the
paratroopers were scattered at the drop. But they did much to
disrupt German defenses behind Utah Beach, justifying
Eisenhower's decision to go ahead with the drop despite Leigh-
Mallory's dire warnings beforehand. Afterwards, the Allied Air
Commander admitted that Eisenhower had been right.

The actions of the 101st Airborne Division are described by
George E. Koskimaki in his book, D-DAY WITH THE
SCREAMING EAGLES [281]. A collection of eyewitness nar-
ratives by 518 participants in the 101st Airborne Division,
Koskimaki's book is praised by military historian S. L. A. Mar-
shall as the best account of the invasion from the airborne soldier's
standpoint. See also Leonard Rapport and Arthur Northwood,
Jr., RENDEZVOUS WITH DESTINY: A HISTORY OF THE
101ST AIRBORNE DIVISION [396], and Donald Burgett,
CURRAHEE! "WE STAND ALONE!" A PARATROOPER'S
ACCOUNT OF THE NORMANDY INVASION [78]. Burgett
served in the 506th Regiment. He writes that the Troop Carrier
Command pulled a "big snafu in Normandy."

The deeds of the 82nd Airborne Division are recounted by its
divisional commander, Matthew B. Ridgway in his book, SOL-

DIER: THE MEMOIRS OF MATTHEW B. RIDGWAY [403]. Clay Blair's, RIDGWAY'S PARATROOPERS: THE AMERI- CAN AIRBORNE IN WORLD WAR II [46] is an excellent account. The assistant divisional commander of the 82nd on D-Day was James M. Gavin who later wrote the superb memoir, ON TO BERLIN [182]. See also Gavin's article, "Back Door to Normandy," published in *Infantry Journal* [183]. Other accounts of the 82nd Airborne are W. Forrest Dawson, SAGA OF THE ALL AMERICAN [123], and Henry L. Covington, A FIGHT- ING HEART: AN UNOFFICIAL STORY OF THE 82ND AIR- BORNE [111]. The 82nd suffered 57 percent casualties in Normandy.

Military historian S. L. A. Marshall's NIGHT DROP: THE AMERICAN AIRBORNE INVASION OF NORMANDY [326] is a detailed account of the airborne assault. See also James A. Huston's OUT OF THE BLUE: U.S. ARMY AIRBORNE OP- ERATIONS IN WORLD WAR II [250].

On the extreme right flank of the Allied landings, in the American sector, the amazing exploits of James Rudder's Rangers in scaling the sheer cliffs of the Pointe du Hoc are described by Ronald L. Lane, RUDDER'S RANGERS [288]. The Germans came to the edge and rolled hand grenades down on the Rangers. Four of the 155mm guns had actually been moved by the enemy, but the Rangers found and destroyed them and then held on for two and a half days until relieved. An eyewitness account is given by G. K. Hodenfield, "I Climbed the Cliffs with the Rangers," *The Saturday Evening Post*. Ranger actions on D-Day are re- viewed by Charles H. Taylor in SMALL UNIT ACTIONS [472], part of the American Forces in Action series.

French Resistance

French Resistance fighters played an important role in delaying the arrival of German reinforcements at the Normandy front. Eisenhower paid tribute to their contribution after the Liberation. In his book, DAS REICH. THE MARCH OF THE 2ND SS

PANZER DIVISION THROUGH FRANCE [215], Max Hastings describes the activities of the French Resistance. On June 8, the Das Reich Division left Montauban in southern France and began a march that ended 450 miles northward in Normandy more than two weeks later. The trip took two or three times longer than necessary because of partisan harassment. Reprisals were forthcoming, the worst occurring in Oradour-sur-Glane where most of the townspeople were massacred.

In his account, FROM MUNICH TO THE LIBERATION, 1938-1944 [20], Frenchman Jean-Pierre Azéma presents a fair-minded view of France on the eve of D-Day, observing that people were afraid that the repeatedly postponed landings would be a fiasco, that German reprisals would increase, and that more French towns would suffer, as many already had under Allied bombing.

General Jacques-Philippe Leclerc's 2nd French Armored Division (2eme Division Blindee), part of General Patton's forces, was committed to action after the St. Lô breakout and was active in the pursuit to the Seine. Veterans of the fighting in Africa, the 2eme Division Blindee was the first French regular division to join with the Anglo-Saxons and the FFI (Forces Francaises de l'Interieure) partisans in the struggle to liberate France. The French division had landed on the Normandy beaches on July 30 without fanfare but created a sensation in the villages and towns through which it passed as Frenchmen caught sight of the tricolor painted on its tanks.

On June 14, General Charles de Gaulle landed in Normandy. His welcome removed doubts as to what the French people felt for him and strengthened his claim to be the legitimate spokesman of France. Despite the author's monumental egotism, de Gaulle's magnificent autobiography provides insights and interpretations on these historic events. See the third volume in his WAR MEMOIRS, entitled SALVATION, 1944-1946 [126].

Henri Michel, the official French historian of the Second World War and editor of the leading journal, *Revue d'histoire de la deuxieme guerre mondiale*, sponsored a colloquiem on World War

II in 1974. The results appeared in a large volume entitled, LA LIBERATION DE LA FRANCE [346]. For the French army, see LES GRANDES UNITÉS FRANCAISES DE LA GUERRE 1939-1945: HISTORIQUES SUCCINCTS, volumes V and VI, edited by Colonel Le Goyet [292]. The invasion of southern France (ANVIL/DRAGOON) on August 15, 1944 relied heavily on French forces commanded by General de Lattre de Tassigny. Much French primary source material is still unavailable to historians.

Genevieve Duboscq, an eleven-year-old Norman girl in 1944 whose house was only five kilometers from Sainte-Mere Eglise, has written her memories of D-Day in her book, MY LONGEST NIGHT [136]. Another eyewitness experience is related by Charles Hargrove in his article, "Quarante Ans Apres," *Revue des Deux Mondes* [208]. A detailed account of the events during the first five hours of D-Day is described by Eddy Florentin in "40eme Anniversaire du Debarquement: Les Cinq Heures H Du Jour," *Historama* [164]. See also M. Baudot, LIBÉRATION DE LA NORMANDIE [28].

Robert Aron, a Gaullist civilian, wrote FRANCE REBORN: THE HISTORY OF THE LIBERATION, JUNE 1944–MAY 1945 [16]. First published in 1959, it is critical of both Montgomery and the Americans. Aron focuses on the operations of the Resistance and the Free French army.

Australian war correspondent, Alan Moorehead, gives his impression of the French reaction to liberation in his book ECLIPSE [361].

OMAHA BEACH

The heaviest losses on D-Day were suffered by the U.S. V Corps that assaulted Omaha Beach, some 2,000 dead, wounded, and missing. The strong German 352nd Division had moved into the Omaha Beach area. Only five of the thirty-two DD (amphibious) tanks—741st Tank Battalion—landed ashore, the rest foundered in the rough seas. In the early hours of D-Day, the invasion

on Omaha Beach bordered on total disaster. The Eisenhower
Library contains the diary of 1st Lt. Jack Shea which is based
largely on the observations of Norman D. Cota, the assistant
divisional commander of the 29th Division. Cota's leadership on
the beaches was critical. The Forrest Pogue combat interviews,
which are now on microfilm, are another important source for
eyewitness accounts.

On the fortieth anniversary of D-Day in 1984, the U.S. Army
reprinted the official account written by Charles H. Taylor,
OMAHA BEACH, 6 JUNE–13 JUNE 1944 [471]. The volume
contains excellent maps and photographs.

The story of the 1st Infantry Division which landed on Omaha
Beach is recounted by H. R. Knickerbocker and others in DAN-
GER FORWARD: THE STORY OF THE FIRST DIVISION IN
WORLD WAR II [280]. Correspondent Don Whitehead describes
the nightmare scenes in a chapter entitled, "As I Saw It." In a
report Whitehead wrote on July 2 for Associated Press, he had
Colonel George Taylor of the 16th Regimental Combat Team, in
a quiet drawl, saying, "Gentlemen, we're being killed here on the
beach, let's move inland and be killed."

The horror—"crimson running tide"— of the first landings is
described by S. L. A. Marshall, "First Wave at Omaha Beach,"
The Atlantic [325]. Perhaps the worst area of the beach, "Dog
Green," was directly in front of strongpoints guarding the
Vierville draw. Within seven minutes of the ramps dropping from
their landing craft, Company A of the 116th, 29th Division, was
decimated. From the cliffs above, the German gunners were
shooting at the survivors as from a roof top.

In three years as a war correspondent, Gordon Gaskill had
never seen such scenes. His graphic account, "Bloody Beach,"
appeared in *American Magazine* [181]. He makes clear that the
landing had been no picnic or anything like a romantic Hollywood
movie.

Naval historian Samuel Elliott Morison considered the best
account written of the invasion written by a passenger in a landing
craft was that by famed war correspondent and writer Ernest

Hemingway. Hemingway's firsthand account, "Voyage to Victory," appeared in *Collier's* [224].

An eyewitness to the naval support offshore was reporter Martin Sommers aboard the destroyer *McCook* commanded by Ralph L. Ramey. Behind *McCook* were the British cruiser *Glasgow* and battleship USS *Texas*. Rear Admiral Carlton F. Bryant, aboard *Texas*, called all destroyers at 0950 hours, "Get on them, men! Get on them! We must knock out those guns! They are raising hell with the men on the beach, and we can't have any more of that! We must stop it!" The action is related by Sommers in "The Longest Hour in History," *The Saturday Evening Post* [452].

From a U.S. Naval vessel close inshore off Normandy, there is the report of W. B. Courtney, "The 100 Hours," *Collier's* [110].

The vital part which naval gunfire played in the Invasion is superbly described by naval writer C. S. Forester, "History's Biggest Gamble," *The Saturday Evening Post* [168]. Many American and Polish destroyers went in as close as 700 yards.

The view from a naval fire control party is told by Coit N. Coker, "Fire Control on Omaha Beach," *Field Artillery Journal* [100].

UTAH BEACH

Losses on Utah Beach were light. By a fortuitous accident, the landing took place more than a mile south of the original beach. Brigadier General Theodore Roosevelt of the 4th Infantry Division, son of a former President, decided to remain where they were and "start the war from here." The U.S. Navy's only major loss on D-Day was the destroyer *Corry*, sunk by a mine.

The official U.S. Army history was written by R. G. Ruppenthal, UTAH BEACH TO CHERBOURG, 6 JUNE–27 JUNE 1944 [416]. For the divisional history of the 4th Infantry that landed at Utah Beach, see Gardner N. Hatch, 4TH INFAN-

TRY "IVY" DIVISION [219]. The Division was in continuous action from June 6 until June 28 and the capture of Cherbourg. During that time, the 4th suffered over 5,450 casualties, with over 800 men killed in action.

OTHER UNITS

The role of the amphibious engineers in unloading supplies over the open beaches at Omaha and Utah is covered in William F. Heavey's DOWN RAMP! THE STORY OF THE ARMY AMPHIBIAN ENGINEERS [222].

The 320th Barrage Balloon Battalion was the only Negro combat unit to take part in the D-Day landings. Men from the unit waded ashore in the early hours of June 6, struggling with their "flying beer bottles" which they had brought across the Channel on the first assault wave. The balloons were intended to deter any low-flying enemy aircraft.

The memories of some other army, navy, and air force personnel who were present on D-Day can be found in Stephen E. Ambrose, "They Were There: D-Day, 1944," *American History Illustrated* [13], and the article, "D-Day Revisited by Five Who Were There," *Armed Forces Journal*.

GOLD, JUNO, AND SWORD BEACHES

The landings on the British beaches, Gold and Sword, are described in the British official history by L. F. Ellis, VICTORY IN THE WEST [150]. The Canadians landed on Juno Beach. The Canadian official history, THE VICTORY CAMPAIGN [456], was written by C. P. Stacey. Published in 1960, Stacey's book is first-rate. Reginald H. Roy's, 1944: THE CANADIANS IN NORMANDY [409], published in 1984, is not afraid to offer criticism where he thinks it is deserved. A popular history with first-class photographs is J. L. Granatstein's, BLOODY VICTORY: CANADIANS AND THE D-DAY CAMPAIGN 1944 [192].

Lt. Col. William T. Barnard's memoir and history, THE QUEEN'S OWN RIFLES OF CANADA, 1860–1960 [25], describes the actions of one of the oldest regiments in the Canadian army during the Normandy campaign. The British 50th Division landed on Gold Beach, see Ewart W. Clay, THE PATH OF THE 50TH [98]. The British 3rd Division landed on Sword Beach, see Norman Scarfe, ASSAULT DIVISION [425], and Robin McNish, IRON DIVISION: THE HISTORY OF THE 3RD DIVISION [338].

The Sherman DD (amphibious) tank, developed by Nicholas Straussler, a Hungarian by birth and British by naturalization, provided important firepower to the assault troops. The British 79th Armoured Division used a variety of specialized armored vehicles. The story of these vehicles is told by Geoffrey Futter, THE FUNNIES: A HISTORY, WITH SCALE PLANS, OF THE 79TH ARMOURED DIVISION [176].

For game players, the John Prados article, "Monty's D-Day: The British and the Normandy Invasion," in Strategy and Tactics [388], is helpful. If the reader is planning to visit Normandy, the article "Normandy, 1944, 1973," published in After the Battle, includes then-and-now photographs accompanied by a text.

Chapter 8

THE BATTLE FOR NORMANDY

INTRODUCTION

D-Day had been a stunning success. The Allies were ashore. But the Invasion had been no more than the first round, the first twenty-four hours in what would be a long drawn-out battle, and success not a foregone conclusion. After June 6, the great battles were still to come. Seven weeks after the invasion, the Germans had twenty-six divisions in Normandy to face the Allies, thirty-four. As the Allies were on the offensive, their superiority on the ground was only marginal.

During those seven weeks, the Allies had only taken as much ground as the invasion planners had envisioned falling in just five days! The stalemate in Normandy soon led to controversy. Ground forces commander Montgomery became the center of this dispute. Eisenhower appealed to Churchill "to persuade Monty to get on his bicycle and start moving." Deputy Supreme Commander Tedder would push for Montgomery's removal. More recently, historians would fault Allied tactics and lack of fighting spirit. The Normandy campaign is prolific in controversies.

In Normandy, Allied soldiers found themselves fighting not only first-class panzer divisions equipped with Panther and Tiger tanks, but up against some of the best armed infantry in the world who were fighting in ideal defensive terrain under leaders who were battle hardened from combat on the Eastern front. Only Allied air power helped to tip the scales against the enemy. American, British, Canadian, Polish, and troops from other Allied nations, as well as German soldiers, with few exceptions on either side, fought with determination, courage, and skill.

On July 25, operation COBRA finally sprung loose the U.S. First Army under General Omar Bradley. St. Lô, like Caen, had finally fallen and the Allies were at last emerging from the hedgerow country onto firm, dry ground. The Allies had suffered 122,000 casualties since the Normandy landing. They had inflicted similar losses on the enemy.

OFFICIAL HISTORIES

The official U.S. Army histories that cover the Normandy campaign are Gordon Harrison's CROSS-CHANNEL ATTACK [212]; Martin Blumenson's, BREAKOUT AND PURSUIT [48]; Forrest Pogue's, THE SUPREME COMMAND [387]; R. G. Ruppenthal's, UTAH BEACH TO CHERBOURG, 6 JUNE–27 JUNE 1944 [416]; Charles H. Taylor, OMAHA BEACH [471]; and David Garth and Charles H. Taylor's ST.-LÔ, 7 JULY–19 JULY 1944 [180]. These volumes touch all aspects of the Normandy campaign, from grand strategy to small unit tactics.

Blumenson rejected Montgomery's claim that the Normandy campaign went according to a "master plan." Blumenson's official volume is extremely hostile to Montgomery, but Blumenson's essay, "Some Reflections on the Immediate Post-Assault Strategy," that appeared in the Eisenhower Foundation book, D-DAY: THE NORMANDY INVASION IN RETRO-SPECT [146], acknowledged that he had been too harsh towards Montgomery.

In THE SUPREME COMMAND, Pogue points out that satisfaction over the initial success gave way to disappointment and criticism. After nearly seven weeks, the deepest penetrations were some twenty-five to thirty miles deep on an eighty-mile front. The frustrations and irritations evaporated for a time when the Allies burst through the enemy lines and swept toward Paris.

The official British history, written by Major L. F. Ellis, VICTORY IN THE WEST: THE BATTLE OF NORMANDY [150], appeared in 1962. Ellis is careful to point out that, vast as was the effort in the West, it was exceeded by the Soviet Union in the East. The enemy are also praised: "Not many troops in the world would have stood the hammering these received and endured so stoutly or so long." The author takes the middle ground over whether Montgomery dawdled at Caen or set a sticky trap for German armor there.

Michael Howard wrote an insightful review essay of the official history for *The Listener*, entitled "The Battle of Normandy" [241]. The battles before the breakout, Howard wrote, showed how much the Allies still had to learn from the Germans about fighting. It is only right, he concluded, that Montgomery should be given chief credit for the campaign's triumphant success.

Air Marshal Sir Philip Wigglesworth, formerly a senior air officer with AEAF and definitely not an admirer of Montgomery, wrote a much more hostile review of the official British history in the RUSI Journal [519].

Military historian Carlo D'Este is also scathing in his criticism of Ellis's official history—"a marvel of obfuscation," "a sanitized and misleading interpretation" are some of the words that D'Este uses to describe Ellis's treatment of the action at Villers Bocage.

The Canadian official history, THE VICTORY CAMPAIGN [456] by C. P. Stacey, is a superb account of the operations of the 1st Canadian Army. From D-Day through August, the total casualties of the Canadian component of the British 21st Army Group had been 18,444, of which 5,021 were killed. Stacey accepts Montgomery's claim that he always intended to attract the enemy's strength to the British front; however, the Canadian historian believes that Montgomery's claim that everything "went according to plan" was a "considerable exaggeration." For some reason, Stacey observes, generals are reluctant to admit that they have made changes or adjustments to fit the new circumstances of a campaign.

GERMAN LITERATURE

The standard reference work for German operations in the Normandy campaign is by Dieter Ose, entitled ENTSCHEIDUNG IM WESTEN, 1944 ("Decision in the West") [377]. He makes it clear that the idea of a second landing persisted well into August. The seventh volume of the German official history of World War II (Das Deutsche Reich und der Zweite Weltkrieg), when published, will cover the operations in Normandy. Other works include F. Helmdach, INVASION IN FRANKREICH IM JUNI 1944 ("Invasion in France in June 1944") [223]; R. Mennel, DIE SCHLUBPHASE DES ZWEITEN WELTKRIEGES IM WESTEN ("The End Phase of the Second World War in the West") [342]; W. Schaufelberger, "OVERLORD: DIE LANDUNG DER WESTALLUERTEN ("Overlord: The Landing of the Western Allies") [426]; P. E. Schramm, DIE INVASION 1944 [430]; H. Wegmuller, DIE ABWEHR DER INVASION: DIE KONZEPTION DES OB WEST, 1940–1944 ("The Defense of the Invasion: The Conception of OB West") [504]; and a University of Cologne doctoral dissertation by J. Ludewig, RUCKZUG DES WESTHEERES VON DER FRANZOSISCHEN WEST–UND SUDKUSTE UND DIE NOCHMALIGE STABILISIERUNG DER WESTFRONT ("The Retreat of the Western Army from the West and South Coast of France and the Repeated Stabilization of the Western Front") [311].

GENERAL HISTORIES

Two recent books by former Sandhurst (War Studies department at the British Military Academy) historians are John

Keegan's, THE SECOND WORLD WAR [268] and H. P. Willmott's, THE GREAT CRUSADE: A NEW COMPLETE HISTORY OF THE SECOND WORLD WAR [520]. Keegan's book is immensely readable and contains one chapter on OVER- LORD. Willmott focuses far more on the Eastern front. Willmott blames what he terms "an ethnocentric consideration of history" for what he considers to be the excessive attention given to the U.S.-British war effort in 1944. The standard survey of the British army is Correlli Barnett's, BRITAIN AND HER ARMY [26]. His treatment of the Normandy campaign is filled with thought-provoking comparisons. He likens the Normandy cam- paign to Passchendaele plus tanks and air power. Given the strength of the enemy's front, Barnett takes the position that there was, as in 1917, "no easy way through."

On the twentieth anniversary of D-Day, Alexander McKee vividly described the fighting that summer of 1944 in his book, CAEN: ANVIL OF VICTORY [335]. Based on the personal accounts of those who fought on both sides, McKee wrote a first-rate narrative of the battle for that city which he said was waged with a "ruthless desperation" with no parallel anywhere outside Russia.

Major General H. Essame, who commanded a British infantry brigade during the Normandy campaign, authored NORMANDY BRIDGEHEAD [157], an excellent, highly readable account of the campaign. See also Eversley Belfield and Brig. H. Essame, THE BATTLE FOR NORMANDY [35].

The campaign is seen through the eyes of a corps commander in Sir Brian Horrocks, CORPS COMMANDER [239].

A different approach is taken by John Keegan in his book, SIX ARMIES IN NORMANDY [269], which focuses on what he perceives to be the national characteristics of the six armies engaged in the campaign. The account is extremely readable although there are some surprising comments. Keegan writes: "every place on the Atlantic Wall was a weak one." He also characterizes the German 352nd behind Omaha Beach as "weak."

H. P. Willmott's book, JUNE 1944 [521], discusses the events that occurred in both Europe and the Far East during the month of June. The author discusses what he calls "The Flaw in Overlord."

The book by the distinguished general Sir William Jackson, "OVERLORD": NORMANDY 1944 [254], is a well-written account of the thirty-month-long invasion debate.

Another useful account is Shelford Bidwell and D. Graham, FIREPOWER: BRITISH ARMY WEAPONS AND THEORIES OF WAR 1904–1945 [43].

The ever-provocative David Irving's, THE WAR BETWEEN THE GENERALS [252], dwells excessively on the personal clashes between Allied generals. Another provocative account is John Ellis's, BRUTE FORCE: ALLIED STRATEGY AND TACTICS IN THE SECOND WORLD WAR [149]. The book is dedicated to showing the incompetence of most Allied commanders.

BRADLEY'S U.S. 1ST ARMY

General Omar Bradley, commander of the U.S. 1st Army, faced a tough assignment in Normandy. A seventeen-day advance of seven miles west of the Vire River and a bare four miles east of it, cost 40,000 U.S. casualties. Added to the ordeal of fighting in ideal defensive country, it was the wettest summer in forty-four years. The terrain of the Cotentin canalized all advances into narrow corridors, preventing Bradley from striking a blow with more than one corps at a time. The American ordeal was reminiscent of Grant's Wilderness campaign. The battles of the bocage are recounted in detail in Blumenson's BREAKOUT AND PURSUIT [48]. In addition to Bradley's own memoirs, there is Charles Whiting's concise, BRADLEY [518].

An excellent account of the entire Northwest Europe campaign is Russell F. Weigley's, EISENHOWER'S LIEUTENANTS [506]. His article, "From the Normandy Beaches to the Falaise-Argentan Pocket," that appeared in the *Military Review* [508], argues that a series of flawed operational decisions contributed to the lengthening of the war.

Highly critical of the U.S. officer corps is Martin Van Creveld's study, FIGHTING POWER: GERMAN AND U.S. ARMY PERFORMANCE, 1939-1945 [493]. He claims that the best and brightest became pen-pushers and the fighting arms were starved of high-quality manpower.

Quality was never in doubt in the case of General Clarence Huebner, commander of the 1st Infantry Division during the Normandy campaign. Martin Blumenson and J. L. Stokesbury, in their book, MASTERS OF THE ART OF COMMAND [52], consider Huebner one of the finest American combat officers of World War II.

Another outstanding combat leader was J. Lawton Collins, commander of the VII Corps in Normandy. Collins, who wrote his autobiography, LIGHTNING JOE [103], had fought on the pestilent southwest Pacific island of Guadalcanal. He compared Normandy fighting with that on Guadalcanal.

The twenty-four-day battle from Utah Beach to the capture of Cherbourg—the port Hitler had decreed must be held at all costs—is described in William B. Breuer's HITLER'S FORTRESS CHERBOURG: THE CONQUEST OF A BASTION [67].

Glover S. Johns, Jr., has an excellent account entitled, THE CLAY PIGEONS OF ST. LÔ [257]. A fresh, detailed, personal history of the fighting in Normandy can be found in Charles R. Cawthon's, OTHER CLAY: A REMEMBRANCE OF THE WORLD WAR II INFANTRY [87]. Cawthon was a company commander in the 2nd Battalion, 116th Infantry Regiment ("Stonewall Brigade"), 29th Division. His article, "July, 1944: St. Lô," in *American Heritage* [86], relates the story of Major Tom Howie, "the Major of St. Lô," who was killed in the battle and whose body was placed in front of the town's shattered cathedral.

The bloody progress of the 29th Division, from D-Day to the capture of St. Lô, is told by Joseph Balkoski in his book,

BEYOND THE BEACHHEAD: THE TWENTY-NINTH IN-
FANTRY IN NORMANDY [23]. An excellent unit history, the
author provides an interesting comparison between American and
German infantry. The Normandy hedgerow fighting required new tactics. The
reaction of the U.S. First Army to this challenge is analyzed by
Captain Michael D. Doubler in his study, BUSTING THE
BOCAGE: AMERICAN COMBINED ARMS OPERATIONS IN
FRANCE, 6 JUNE-31 JULY 1944 [135]. In the Normandy
fighting, combined arms coordination was necessary but not
always present. Doubler mentions instances of violent outbursts
between tankers and infantrymen.

Reminiscent of the Wilderness Campaign of 1864 or World
War I battles, in the bocage fighting of July 1944 a 100-yard gain
often meant a whole day's work for a battalion. An eyewitness
account is provided by Colonel Gerden F. Johnson in his HIS-
TORY OF THE TWELFTH INFANTRY REGIMENT IN
WORLD WAR II [258].

The experience of a combat engineer is described in the memoir
of Colonel David E. Pergrin, FIRST ACROSS THE RHINE:
THE 291ST ENGINEER COMBAT BATTALION IN FRANCE,
BELGIUM, AND GERMANY [381].

In preparation for the fiftieth anniversary of the Normandy
campaign, William M. Hammond, a historian with the U.S. Army
Center of Military History, has a forthcoming publication entitled, OVERLORD: THE NORMANDY INVASION, FROM
THE LANDING TO ST. LÔ [206].

U.S. divisional histories include Robert L. Hewitt's, WORK
HORSE OF THE WESTERN FRONT: THE STORY OF THE
30TH INFANTRY DIVISION [226] (the "Old Hickory" Division
helped to stop Hitler's counterattack at Mortain in August); Joe
I. Abrams's A HISTORY OF THE 90TH DIVISION IN WORLD
WAR II, 6 JUNE 1944 TO 9 MAY 1945 [1]; and Joseph B.
Mittelman's, EIGHT STARS TO VICTORY: A HISTORY OF
THE VETERAN NINTH U.S. INFANTRY DIVISION [356].
These and other unit histories may be found at the U.S. Army

Military History Institute, Carlisle Barracks, Pennsylvania. An important primary source is the First U.S. Army, REPORT OF OPERATIONS [162], which consists of seven volumes covering the Normandy campaign.

MONTGOMERY

General Bernard L. Montgomery commanded the Allied ground forces or 21st Army Group during the Normandy campaign. Under his command were the 1st U.S. Army commanded by Omar Bradley, made up of the VII and V Corps, and the 2nd British Army commanded by Miles Dempsey, made up of the XXX and 1st Corps.

Much admired and much detested, both then and now, "Monty" has figured large in virtually every account of the Normandy campaign. Among the earliest general accounts that covered Normandy operations were Chester Wilmot's, THE STRUGGLE FOR EUROPE [522], John North's, NORTHWEST EUROPE, 1944–1945: THE ACHIEVEMENT OF 21ST ARMY GROUP [375], and Milton Shulman's, DEFEAT IN THE WEST [438]. All three books were exceptionally well-researched, eminently readable, and were in many ways a reply to what Canadian historian Shulman called the "recent carping criticism about the conduct of the battle of Caen." All three books accepted Montgomery's claim that his master plan for the battle of Normandy had been to attract to the anvil of Caen the bulk of German armor and there methodically hammer it to pieces. Critics have referred to this interpretation as the "21st Army School of History."

Montgomery's position was made crystal clear with the publication of his memoirs in 1958, THE MEMOIRS OF FIELD MARSHAL THE VISCOUNT MONTGOMERY OF ALAMEIN, K.G. [358]. "I never once had cause or reason to alter my master plan," he wrote, which was to draw German armor on to the 2nd British Army front, so that Bradley's 1st Army could break out on the western flank. Montgomery criticized

Eisenhower for failing to understand the plan. Montgomery blamed General Frederick Morgan (Deputy Chief of Staff, SHAEF) for much of the problem since he considered Eisenhower "a god" while placing "me (Monty) at the other end of the celestial ladder." Morgan, he said, was supported by the airmen, Coningham and Tedder.

Michael Howard reviewed Montgomery's memoirs for THE NEW STATESMAN [242]. Under the title, "The Field-Marshal," Howard discusses Montgomery's many strengths, including his professionalism and unshakable self-confidence, as well as his many weaknesses, among them tactlessness, conceit, and inability to serve as a number-two man. A team player he was not.

As noted previously, the official U.S. Army volume written by Martin Blumenson was highly critical of Montgomery. The depths of that hostility was reached in Blumenson's 1962 article, "The Most Overrated General of World War II," that appeared in the professional military journal *Armor* [51]. Facing the title page was a large photograph of Montgomery! At that time (the author later modified his view), Blumenson regarded Montgomery as merely "competent, adequate."

Far more balanced was Blumenson's volume on the Normandy campaign published by Time-Life Books in 1978 entitled, LIBERATION [50]. The author's narrative, aided by excellent photographs, elaborates on the difficulties encountered in the campaign, as well as noting that 586 towns and villages in Normandy (like Caen and St. Lô) had to be rebuilt following liberation.

American military historian Charles B. MacDonald wrote an excellent account of the campaign in northwest Europe entitled, THE MIGHTY ENDEAVOR: AMERICAN ARMED FORCES IN THE EUROPEAN THEATER IN WORLD WAR II [316]. The title comes from President Roosevelt's message on D-Day. Perhaps the author's view of Montgomery may be gauged from the fact that he compares Monty's behavior after D-Day with that of General John P. Lucas at Anzio.

Montgomery's strategy in the Battle of Normandy was vigorously defended by the former head of his operations and planning staff, Major General David Belchem in his book, VICTORY IN NORMANDY [34]. Belchem was an apologist until his death in July 1981 for Monty's "all went according to plan" school of thought. The book is a valuable first-hand account of the Normandy campaign.

Generally favorable to Montgomery is the study by Richard Lamb, MONTGOMERY IN EUROPE, 1943-1945: SUCCESS OR FAILURE? [285]. Lamb accepts the "master plan" thesis. Lamb writes that on D-Day traffic congestion on the beaches was far greater than anticipated, thus preventing Montgomery's armored thrusts from penetrating deep inland and quickly on June 6. On June 9, Montgomery had wanted to drop an airborne division south of Caen. Leigh-Mallory vetoed the plan. Montgomery wrote to his chief of staff: "Obviously he [Leigh-Mallory] is a gutless bugger who refused to take a chance and plays for safety on all occasions. I have no use for him." He later changed his view of the Allied Air Commander.

The second volume of Nigel Hamilton's monumental biography of Montgomery, MASTER OF THE BATTLEFIELD: MONTY'S WAR YEARS, 1942-1944 [205], was commended by reviewers Paul Fussell and Edward Luttwak for illuminating Montgomery's character. At the same time, however, both Fussell and Luttwak detected a tone of hagiography in the book. Hamilton was Monty's close friend and admirer.

Hamilton is particularly condemnatory of Tedder, whose effort to get Montgomery dismissed the biographer calls "one of the most reprehensible performances by a senior Allied commander in modern battle history."

Russell Weigley felt there was not quite enough of the "acrid smell of cordite" about Hamilton's biography. Yet Weigley notes that the biography has done much to dispel the widespread notion that Montgomery was simply an unimaginative plodder.

Montgomery-bashing books include those by J. J. How, NORMANDY: THE BRITISH BREAKOUT [240]; Richard Rohmer,

PATTON'S GAP: AN ACCOUNT OF THE BATTLE OF NOR-
MANDY 1944 [404]; and John Ellis, BRUTE FORCE [149].
How faults Montgomery for failing to seize the town of Vire, a
key road junction in the rear of the German 7th Army, on August
2; Rohmer's account is a diatribe and based on flimsy evidence;
Ellis, who emphasizes the material superiority of the Allies,
claims that "a press hungry for heroes" made Montgomery and
Patton merely seem like great commanders.

CARLO D'ESTE

In 1983 appeared Carlo D'Este's masterly DECISION IN
NORMANDY [128]. In this his first book, D'Este echoed the
words of Basil Liddell Hart that there had been too much
glorification and too little investigation of the Normandy campaign. His stated purpose was to separate the truth from the
mythology of the Normandy campaign. He achieved astonishing
success, writing one of the best narrative and analytical accounts
of the Normandy campaign. Old questions were resolved and
new ones raised in D'Este's fresh interpretation of the personalities and issues of the Battle of Normandy.

New York *Times* military correspondent Drew Middleton, who
in 1944 was a war correspondent attached to Allied headquarters,
called DECISION IN NORMANDY "the best-researched, best-
reasoned, best-written account of that campaign." D'Este's book
was also well received in Britain where the reviewer for *The
Economist* commented that the account "is surprisingly pro-
Montgomery for a work by a retired American lieutenant-colonel." Other books by Carlo D'Este have followed since, leading
Montgomery biographer Nigel Hamilton to refer to the retired
lieutenant-colonel as "the finest historian of the Second World
War in the West."

Perhaps after nearly half a century, D'Este has laid to rest the
controversy surrounding Montgomery's "master plan." In one
way the book is an indictment of Montgomery since the author
conclusively demonstrates that only *after* the failure to take Caen

did Montgomery emphasize 2nd Army's *defensive* role in acting as a magnet for German armor. Montgomery did not get to Caen. Failure to take Caen, D'Este writes, was not just a "local setback," but a major failure. At the same time, D'Este is not a Montgomery-basher, and he acknowledges the adaptability of Montgomery when the unknown intervened to force a change in his original plans and he was forced to improvise. Eventually, the Germans were to concentrate seven armored divisions or two-thirds of their armor in France on a twenty-mile front facing the British 2nd Army.

DECISION IN NORMANDY, however, is much more than a reappraisal of Montgomery in Normandy. D'Este singles out the British army for a detailed examination. He exonerates from blame the British 3rd Division for failing to take Caen on D-Day—the presence of the 21st Panzer Division makes such criticism unfair, he writes. He does believe, however, that the Normandy campaign demonstrated the war-weariness of the British army, at least certain units in it. The author mentions that some U.S. units also experienced problems in Normandy.

His grasp of the sources and ability to capture high drama are also apparent in his account of the battle at Villers-Bocage on June 13, when the spearhead of the British 7th Armoured Division (Desert Rats) attempted to outflank the Panzer Lehr Division. Within five minutes, the panzer ace Michael Wittmann, in his lone Tiger, a 55-ton steel monster, destroyed the lead elements of a British armored brigade. This, writes D'Este, was "one of the most decisive moments in the battle of Normandy." Bucknall, the XXX Corps commander, eventually withdrew the 7th Armoured from Villers-Bocage. D'Este feels that a reinforced 7th Armoured Division could have resumed the offensive, and he faults Monty for placing Bucknall in command of the XXX Corps in the first place.

D'Este's chapter on "The Manpower Dilemma" raises new questions since he claims that the evidence available (he says the relevant War Office papers in the PRO are missing and he explains his difficulties in trying to locate them) suggests that the infantry

shortage which plagued Montgomery was in fact a myth. D'Este
contends that there were over 100,000 infantry replacements
available within Britain itself. Did Churchill withhold them from
Normandy, he asks?

"OLD SOLDIERS UNDER FIRE"

"Our tactics, our training, above all our morale are minutely
examined by generals, by writers, by correspondents to *The
Times*," lamented a former British Eighth Army officer in a letter
of his own to *The Times* in 1959. Self-doubt about the British
army's fighting ability went back to the war itself when failures
in the Middle East and Far East were attributed to class-conscious-
ness, incompetent officers, or "softness" as a result of democracy.

The capabilities of the Allied armies in Normandy were
examined by Max Hastings in his popular fortieth anniversary
study, OVERLORD: D-DAY AND THE BATTLE OF NOR-
MANDY [216], published in 1984. He concluded that British and
American soldiers had neither the dedication nor the professional
skill of the Germans. For examples of endurance and sacrifice,
the author concluded that it would be necessary to look to the
example of the German army and the "extraordinary defense its
men conducted in Europe in the face of all the odds against them."

Hastings's criticism of the Allied military performance in
Normandy is echoed by John Ellis in his book BRUTE FORCE
[149]. Any comparison between the Allied armies and their
opponents, Ellis writes, can only be "invidious."

An ambitious project that seeks to examine the military effectiveness of all the major participants in World Wars I and II is the
three-volume series, MILITARY EFFECTIVENESS [353], edited by military historians Allan R. Millett and Williamson
Murray. Grades are assigned to the various national armies for
tactical and operational performance. Millett states that the
American army was a "flawed instrument" that often compen-
sated for operational flaws with logistical abundance. Millett,
however, gives the U.S. army a B in tactical performance. The

British army receives only mediocre grades. The Germans earn an A in tactical performance. The study, writes Paul Halpern, is a worthwhile addition to military history in the twentieth century. While praise is generally heaped upon the Wehrmacht, H. P. Willmott, in his recent book, THE GREAT CRUSADE [520], takes issue with those whom he regards as "obsessed with the pernicious myth of German military excellence, of which the defence of Normandy is held to be an example." In assessing performance in Normandy, Willmott writes that the proper context is not selective consideration of one single part of the campaign but by a comparison of the 1940 and 1944 campaigns. He believes that the 1944 Normandy campaign compares very favorably with the earlier Wehrmacht campaign in 1940.

The combat effectiveness of the First Canadian Army is analyzed in the 1991 book by John A. English, THE CANADIAN ARMY AND THE NORMANDY CAMPAIGN: A STUDY OF FAILURE IN HIGH COMMAND [153]. A long-serving infantry and staff officer in the Canadian land forces, English based his account upon a reading of the records in the Canadian Department of National Defence and personal papers in the National Archives of Canada.

Operation SPRING, the code name for the Canadian attack on July 25, was the worst day of the war for Canadians, except for Dieppe. The assault by the Canadian Black Watch battalion was like the Charge of the Light Brigade or Pickett's charge at Gettysburg. While finding the First Canadian Army brave "beyond dispute," the author finds fault with the Canadian high command. In his Foreword to the book, historian Gunther E. Rothenberg thinks English has "made his case."

The bitter fighting of the Normandy campaign was reflected not only in killed and wounded but also in the number of battle exhaustion cases. Canadian historians Terry Copp and Bill McAndrew have written the valuable study, BATTLE EXHAUSTION: SOLDIERS AND PSYCHIATRISTS IN THE CANADIAN ARMY, 1939–1945 [109]. Using a cross-disciplinary approach that makes useful connections between the armed services, war studies, history and medicine, the study is an investigation into the incidence of breakdown and its treatment among Canadian troops. See also R. H. Ahrenfeldt, PSYCHIA-TRY IN THE BRITISH ARMY IN THE SECOND WORLD WAR [3], and an article by Lt. Col. A. T. A. Browne, "A Study of the Anatomy of Fear and Courage in War," in *The Army Quarterly & Defence Journal* [73].

The British 3rd Division has been described as being given the most ambitious, most difficult, and most important task of all the units that landed on D-Day, namely the capture of Caen. It was later criticized, by Chester Wilmot in particular, for what was described as a disappointing performance. Lt. Col. Eric T. Lummis, who landed with the 1st Battalion Suffolk Regiment, 3rd Division, defends their actions in his article, "D-Day, 6 June 1944: The Truth About 3rd British Division," in *Army Quarterly & Defence Journal* [312].

J. B. Salmud, in his book, THE HISTORY OF THE 51ST HIGHLAND DIVISION, 1939–1945 [420], admits that not all was well with this veteran British 8th Army division in the early days of the campaign. Sir Martin Lindsay, who commanded 1st Bn. Gordon Highlanders (51st Highland Division), has an article, "The Young and the Brave—Morale in Battle," in *Army Quarterly & Defence Journal* [305]. He notes that they were puzzled by the comparatively poor performance of the three battle-experienced formations in the early days of the Normandy campaign.

The renowned 7th Armoured Division is also one of the Desert units that has been accused of being "sticky" during initial encounters with the enemy in Normandy. The most recent study of that famed unit is by Robin Neillands, THE DESERT RATS: 7TH ARMOURED DIVISION, 1940–1945 [369].

Stephen Badsey's book, NORMANDY 1944: ALLIED LANDINGS AND BREAKOUT [21] is a concise account de-signed for wargamers. He suggests that Allied infantry could not have been as bad as they said they were in Normandy combat.

The courage and skill of the German troops is praised in Brigadier C. N. Barclay's memoir, THE HISTORY OF THE

53RD (WELSH) DIVISION IN THE SECOND WORLD WAR
[24]. By the time the 53rd Division arrived in Normandy at the
end of June, the "slogging match" on the left flank was in full
swing. The German opposition confronted by the Allies is described
by Ashley Brown and Jonathan Reed in THE ARMOUR [72] and
by Craig W. H. Luther in his book, BLOOD AND HONOR:
THE HISTORY OF THE 12TH SS PANZER DIVISION "HIT-
LER YOUTH," 1943-1945 [314]. The elite 12th SS Panzer
Division Hitlerjugend (Hitler Youth), many of its troops under
the age of eighteen, was characterized by reckless determination
combined with fanaticism and self-sacrifice. It was led by the
battle-hardened Kurt Meyer who had learned his craft on the
Eastern front. After the war, Meyer was convicted of war crimes
by a Canadian court and sentenced to death. He was eventually
released due to ill health and died shortly afterwards. The worst
incident occurred at Chateau Audrieu, where a unit of the 12th
SS shot nearly forty Canadian and British prisoners against a
stone wall. From that time on, little quarter was given on either
side in engagements between the Canadian 3rd Division and the
12th SS.

THE AIR FORCES IN NORMANDY

The role of the British and American air forces during the
ground campaign in Normandy is just as controversial as that
before D-Day. In their memoirs and written accounts, Allied
soldiers frequently described the air contribution to victory as
"magnificent"—weather permitting, that is. Major General H.
Essame, a veteran infantry commander and an exceptionally
observant commentator on the war, was probably not alone in
feeling some bitterness toward British airmen who had the
"normal flatulence of the office-bound military bureaucrat." The
literature on the Montgomery—Tedder/army-air force dispute
has continued to be rancorous. U.S. army-air force relations were
less antagonistic.

On the subject of close air support, there is an Air Command and Staff College study by Major Michael L. Wolfert, FROM ACTS TO COBRA: EVOLUTION OF CLOSE AIR SUPPORT DOCTRINE IN WORLD WAR TWO [528]. Wolfert justifiably credits Major General Elwood R. Quesada, commander of Ninth Tactical Air Force, for assuring better CAS for American ground troops. The case for the effectiveness of Anglo-American air support in Normandy is ably presented by Richard P. Hallion in his book, STRIKE FROM THE SKY: THE HISTORY OF BATTLEFIELD AIR ATTACK, 1911–1945 [203].

Standard accounts on the air war in Normandy are Craven and Cate, THE ARMY AIR FORCES IN WORLD WAR II, VOL. III, EUROPE: ARGUMENT TO V-E DAY, JANUARY 1944 TO MAY 1945 [112] and D. Richards and H. St. G. Saunders, THE ROYAL AIR FORCE, 1939–1945 [401].

Military historian John Terraine, the main champion in contemporary historical writing of World War I general Douglas Haig, published in 1985 a history of the British Air Force entitled, A TIME FOR COURAGE: THE ROYAL AIR FORCE IN THE EUROPEAN WAR, 1939–1945 [475]. Pro-Tedder and Coningham, Terraine uses words like "specious," "ridiculous," and "absurd" in describing Montgomery's actions. He argues that the poor fighting quality of the British army "threw ever-increasing burdens on the airmen."

From the perspective of an army participant, there is the memoir of Charles Carrington whose job during the war is indicated by the title of his book, SOLDIER AT BOMBER COMMAND [84]. Despite what the author refers to as "Air Force insolence," close air support operations in Normandy showed "a marked improvement." Military historian and reviewer Brian Bond noted that Carrington's book fills an important gap in the historiography of World War II. Also on the subject of air-ground tactical cooperation is Christopher Chant's, GROUND ATTACK [93].

On the controversial subject of the effectiveness of the rocket-firing Typhoon as an anti-tank weapon, there is an article by

Alfred Price, "The 3-Inch Rocket: How Effective Was It Against the German Tanks in Normandy?" *The Royal Air Forces Quarterly* [390].

OPERATION GOODWOOD

One of the most debated battles of the Normandy campaign was Operation GOODWOOD. Launched on July 18, the new offensive was intended to clear the way into the open country that led to Paris. Preceded by the heaviest "carpet" bombardment of the war (over 7,000 tons of bombs), GOODWOOD involved all three British armored divisions in Normandy. Montgomery declared that "My whole eastern flank will burst into flames," and he said the operation "may have far-reaching results." After nearly 2,000 Allied planes had dropped their bombs, the British armored divisions advanced well in the morning, but were brought to a standstill in the afternoon by antitank fire and armored counterattacks. By evening of the 20th, the British forces had come to a halt. The British lost 450 tanks in GOODWOOD. Eisenhower was "livid" over GOODWOOD and Tedder pushed for Montgomery's removal. If GOODWOOD failed to achieve a breakout, the offensive had pulled German armored reserves toward the British front, and by the end of July the perimeter drawn around the Allied bridgehead was stretched close to breaking point.

GOODWOOD is described by Alexander McKee in his book, CAEN: ANVIL OF VICTORY [335]; John T. Sweet examines the battle in MOUNTING THE THREAT: THE BATTLE OF BOURGUEBUS RIDGE [470]. The Bourguebus Ridge was the stretch of high ground that served to block the British drive toward the road to Paris. The controversy over GOODWOOD is discussed in D'Este's DECISION IN NORMANDY [128]; Butcher's MY THREE YEARS WITH EISENHOWER [80]; Ambrose's THE SUPREME COMMANDER [12]; Tedder's WITH PREJUDICE [473]; Chandler's EISENHOWER PAPERS [91]; and Bryant's TRIUMPH IN THE WEST [76].

The regimental commander of the 21st Panzer Division, Hans von Luck, describes his actions on Bourguebus Ridge in his memoir, PANZER COMMANDER: THE MEMOIRS OF COLONEL HANS VON LUCK [310]. He arrived on the battlefield straight from Paris and hastily coordinated a defense. GOODWOOD tank operations are also discussed by Liddell Hart in volume two of his work, THE TANKS [302].

OPERATION COBRA

Operation COBRA was the code name given to the First U.S. Army effort to break out of the Normandy hedgerows. St. Lô fell to Major General Charles H. Corlett's XIX Corps on July 18-19. Defending against the Americans was German General Paul Hausser's Seventh Army, consisting of LXXXIV Corps in the COBRA sector and II Parachute Corps in the vicinity of Caumont.

General Omar Bradley intended to use the heavy bombers to blow a gap in the enemy line through which General Lawton Collins's VII Corps would be pushed, until finally the VIII Corps under George S. Patton, Jr. would burst into the open.

Operations for July 24 were cancelled but too late to prevent 700 tons of bombs being dropped on the target area. A bombing error killed twenty-five soldiers in the U.S. 30th Division. The operation was rescheduled for July 25. Another "short" bombing killed 111 and wounded hundreds in the 30th and 9th Divisions. Lt. General Lesley J. McNair was killed in the bombing shortfall. McNair was the highest ranking Allied officer killed in northwest Europe.

The Eighth and Ninth U.S. Air Forces dropped more than 4,000 tons of explosives on the enemy. In the days that followed the heavy air bombardment, Lawton Collins exploited the gap made in the enemy line. On the other side, what had once been the most powerful armored division in the German army, Panzer Lehr, had been reduced by six weeks of Normandy fighting to a mere fourteen tanks.

Sooner than anyone imagined, the Americans had broken out of the terrible bocage country. The frustrations, disappointments, and recriminations that had marked the Normandy campaign were over, at least for a time. A German counterattack at Mortain would fail disastrously, and the German Seventh Army would soon be destroyed in the Falaise Gap. Hard fighting would lie ahead but the decisive battle in the west had been fought and won by the Allies.

For detailed accounts on COBRA operations see Martin Blumenson, BREAKOUT AND PURSUIT [48]; Omar Bradley, A SOLDIER'S STORY [63]; J. Lawton Collins, LIGHTNING JOE [103]; Russell Weigley, EISENHOWER'S LIEUTENANTS [506]; Lewis H. Brereton, THE BRERETON DIARIES [66]; and John L. Sullivan, "The Botched Air Support of Operation COBRA," *Parameters* [467].

Chapter 9

TRENDS IN FUTURE RESEARCH

As the previous chapters in this historiographical bibliography of the Normandy campaign, 1944, have demonstrated, some topics and areas of the subject have been extensively investigated over the nearly half-century since that epochal event of World War II. The Second Front question, the Transportation Plan, FORTI-TUDE, MULBERRIES, D-Day, and the Battle of Normandy itself have been closely examined. Biographies, strategy, gener-alship, unit histories, and intelligence activities have received the lion's share of researchers' attention. The common soldier, sailor, and airman less so. Historian Stephen Ambrose has noted in connection with the collection of oral histories that "we know pretty much what the top brass did; what we need is the story of the private at Omaha Beach, the sailor on the LST, the fighter pilot overhead, the code-breaker back in England, the factory worker in New Orleans who built the landing craft."

This is not to say that all of the leading figures involved in the Normandy campaign have received adequate treatment since that is not the case. On Eisenhower, we do have Ambrose's own excellent biography, and there is Nigel Hamilton's outstanding study of Montgomery. Russell Weigley has discussed a number of the other commanders in his first-rate study, *Eisenhower's Lieutenants*. Professor Dominick Graham has been commissioned to write the biography of Canadian General Guy Simonds. There remains, however, a need for detailed studies of such figures as Walter Bedell Smith, Tedder, Bradley, Leigh-Mallory, Quesada, as well as other commanders.

The combat performance of Allied armies in Normandy has received particular attention of late, starting perhaps with Max Hasting's *Overlord*, which presented the German army as almost supermen. There is beyond question a need for an up-to-date analysis of the Wehrmacht in Normandy. Such a work or works would examine the motivation of the ordinary German soldier, as well as considering weapons, tactics, and strategy. Recently, Canadian John English has published an analytical study, *The Canadian Army and the Normandy Campaign: A Study in Failure in High Command*. More such works, grounded in research in the military records, are needed for divisions, corps, armies, and air forces.

A word of caution is perhaps in order. During the 1990 meeting of the American Military Institute, a panel of senior historians assessed the present state of scholarship on World War II. Ronald H. Spector observed that writing for the first twenty or thirty years after the war was "essentially celebratory in tone."[1] There was a lot of recounting of heroic deeds and self-justificatory memoirs by participants. Spector notes that within the last five years books on World War II are much more somber, sad, and realistic. Professor of English Paul Fussell's writing expresses perhaps an extreme view of the "new" attitude toward World War II. Besides criticizing what he regards as the trivializing and sanitizing of war in many historical works, he also questions the actual necessity for war.

As historians revise, confirm, or modify what their predecessors have written, there is a need to keep in mind the hope of Michael Howard that they will show "generosity and understanding of the problems and the weaknesses of the people involved."[2]

Bryan Ranft has also reminded us that war is unpredictable: "Is it possible," he writes, "that historians, anxious to find patterns and coherence, are in danger of distancing themselves from reality as experienced by those who fought?"[3] As June 6, 1944, recedes ever further into the mists of time and generations have no personal memory of the Normandy campaign there is both the opportunity for new questions and fresh insights, while at the same time the danger exists of losing touch with the reality of those who experienced D-Day.

An essential means of re-creating the reality or mind-set of those who fought is to have access to all of the information that was available to those at the time. The archives of the era must be opened freely to researchers. The existing closed files in the United States and Britain only serve to fuel the imaginative minds of those who favor conspiratorial explanations for events in history. Although many difficulties remain in accessing Russian records, the opening of secret Soviet files will also shed more light on such questions as the Second Front issue.

Christopher R. Gabel has noted that the logistical debate over the question of whether or not the logistical "tail" was out of proportion to the combat "teeth" is in need of closer examination. Lt.-Gen. John C. H. Lee, who commanded the Services of Supply, is also a figure worthy of treatment. Researchers also need to examine the contributions of various French Resistance groups to the success of the invasion. Gabel's call for a detailed, nonpartisan study of Montgomery's plans for the Normandy Campaign has been answered, as we have seen, by Carlo D'Este's work.

It has been noted, however, that Clio rarely sleeps in the same bed for long; all historical writing is a progress report, and the reputations of political and military leaders are especially prone to revisionist assessment. As we approach the fiftieth anniversary of D-Day, it can be definitely said that the last word on that turning point in the twentieth century has hardly been written. There is an enormous amount of research that has yet to be done on nearly every facet of the Normandy campaign, from those who supplied the necessary equipment and weapons to those who used them, and those who provided medical treatment to the casualties. When the definitive history of the Normandy campaign is eventually written, definitive in the sense of presenting a comprehensive view of that epic event, it is to be hoped that the writer will recall the SHAEF emblem and its meaning: against a black background representing Nazism is a silver sword (of liberation) enveloped in fire. Above the sword is a rainbow representing the colors of the United Nations and above that a solid, pale blue strip signifying the freedom that the Allies would bring to Europe.

NOTES

1. Richard H. Kohn, ed., "The Scholarship on World War II: Its Present Condition and Future Possibilities," *The Journal of Military History* 55 (July 1991): 369.
2. Ibid., 380.
3. Bryan Ranft, *Times Literary Supplement*, September 13, 1991.

PART II

BIBLIOGRAPHY

1. Abrams, Joe I. *A History of the 90th Division in World War II, 6 June 1944 to 9 May 1945*. Baton Rouge: Army Navy Publishing Company, 1946.

2. Ahearn, J. L. "D-Day, June 6, 1944." *Look* 28 (June 16, 1964): 21–23.

3. Ahrenfeldt, R. H. *Psychiatry in the British Army in the Second World War*. London: H.M. Stationary Office, 1958.

4. Alden, Robert. "The Silence of Omaha Beach." *New York Times Magazine* (May 27, 1962): 15+.

5. Allsup, John S. *Hedgerow Hell*. Bayeux: Editions Heimdal, 1985.

6. Ambrose, Stephen E. *Eisenhower: Soldier, General of the Army, President-elect, 1890–1952*. Vol. 1. New York: Simon & Schuster, 1983.

7. Ambrose, Stephen E. "Eisenhower's Generalship." *Parameters: U.S. Army War College Quarterly* 20, no. 2 (June 1990): 2–12.

8. Ambrose, Stephen E. "Eisenhower, the Intelligence Community, and the D-Day Invasion." *Wisconsin Magazine of History* 64, no. 4 (Summer 1981): 261–77.

9. Ambrose, Stephen E. "Eisenhower and the Intelligence Community in World War II." *Journal of Contemporary History* 16 (1979): 153–66.

10. Ambrose, Stephen E. *Pegasus Bridge, June 6, 1944.* New York: Simon & Schuster, 1985.

11. Ambrose, Stephen E. "The Secrets of Overlord." *The Quarterly Journal of Military History* 1, no. 4 (Summer 1989): 70–75.

12. Ambrose, Stephen E. *The Supreme Commander: The War Years of General Dwight D. Eisenhower.* London: Cassell, 1968.

13. Ambrose, Stephen E. "They Were There: D-Day, 1944." *American History Illustrated* 4, no. 3 (June 1969): 4–7.

14. American Heritage. *D-Day, the Invasion of Europe.* New York: American Heritage Publishing Company, 1962.

15. Army Times. *D-Day: The Greatest Invasion.* New York: Putnam, 1969.

16. Aron, Robert. *France Reborn: The History of the Liberation, June 1944–May 1945.* Translated from the French. New York: Scribner's, 1964.

17. Asprey, Robert B. *War in the Shadows.* Garden City, N.Y.: Doubleday, 1975.

18. Assmann, Kurt. "Normandy, 1944." *Military Review* 34 (February 1955): 86–93.

19. Auphan, Paul, and Jacques Mordal. *The French Navy in World War II*. Translated by A. C. I. Sabalot. Annapolis: U.S. Naval Institute, 1959.

20. Azéma, Jean-Pierre. *From Munich to the Liberation, 1938–1944*. Translated by Janet Lloyd. New York: Cambridge University Press, 1984.

21. Badsey, Stephen. *Normandy 1944: Allied Landings and Breakout*. London: Osprey, 1990.

22. Baldwin, Hanson W. "As Eisenhower Sees It Two Years After." *New York Times Magazine* (June 2, 1946): 7–9+.

23. Balkoski, Joseph. *Beyond the Beachhead. The 29th Infantry Division in Normandy*. Harrisburg, Pa.: Stackpole Books, 1989.

24. Barclay, C. N. *The History of the 53rd (Welsh) Division in the Second World War*. London: William Clowes, 1956.

25. Barnard, William T. *The Queen's Own Rifles of Canada, 1860–1960*. Ontario: Ontario Publishing Company, 1960.

26. Barnett, Correlli. *Britain and Her Army, 1509–1970: A Military, Political, and Social Survey*. New York: Morrow, 1970.

27. Barnett, Correlli. *Engage the Enemy More Closely: The Royal Navy in the Second World War*. New York: W. W. Norton, 1991.

28. Baudot, M. *Libération de la Normandie*. Paris: Hachette, 1974.

29. Bayliss, Gwyn M. *Bibliographic Guide to the Two World Wars: An Annotated Survey of English-Language Reference Materials*. New York: Bowker, 1978.

30. Beacham, Edmund G. "The Fortieth Anniversary of D-Day, June 6, 1944: A Physician Remembers." *Maryland State Medical Journal* 33 (June 1984): 450–53.

31. Beaumont, Roger A. *Special Operations and Elite Units, 1939–1988: A Research Guide.* Westport, Conn.: Greenwood, 1988.

32. Beck, Alfred M., et al. *The Technical Services. The Corps of Engineers: The War Against Germany.* Washington, D.C.: Center of Military History, 1985.

33. Bedarida, François, ed. *Normandie 44: Du Debarquement a La Liberation.* Institute d' Histoire du Temps Present. Paris: Albin Michael, 1987.

34. Belchem, David. *Victory in Normandy.* London: Chatto & Windus, 1982.

35. Belfield, E., and H. Essame. *The Battle for Normandy.* London: Batsford, 1983.

36. Benamou, Jean-Pierre. *The Landing Beaches.* Bayeux: Heimdal, 1982.

37. Bennett, Ralph. "Fortitude, Ultra and the 'Need to Know.' " *Intelligence and National Security* 4 (July 1989): 482–502.

38. Bennett, Ralph. *Ultra in the West: The Normandy Campaign of 1944–45.* London: Hutchinson, 1979.

39. Bennett, Ralph. "Ultra and Some Command Decisions." *Journal of Contemporary History* 16, no. 1 (January 1981): 131–51.

40. Bennett, Ralph. *"Ultra" in the West: The Normandy Campaign, 1944–1945.* New York: Scribner, 1980.

41. Bernage, Georges. *The Battle of Normandy: 7 June to 19 August 1944.* Translated by P. L. Jutras. Bayeux: Editions Heimdal, 1984.

42. Bernstein, Barton J. "The Uneasy Alliance: Roosevelt-Churchill and the Atomic Bomb, 1940–1945." *Western Political Quarterly* 29 (1976).

43. Bidwell, Shelford, and Dominick Graham. *Firepower: British Army Weapons and Theories of War, 1904–1945*. London: Unwin Hyman, 1982.

44. Binkoski, Joseph. *The 115th Infantry Regiment in World War Two*. Washington, D.C.: Infantry Journal Press, 1948.

45. Bird, Keith W. *German Naval History: A Guide to the Literature*. New York: Garland, 1985.

46. Blair, Clay. *Ridgway's Paratroopers; the American Airborne in World War II*. Dial Press, 1985.

47. Bliven, Bruce. *Story of D-Day: June 6, 1944*. New York: Random House, 1956.

48. Blumenson, Martin. *Breakout and Pursuit*. U.S. Army in World War II: The European Theater of Operations. Washington, D.C.: Government Printing Office, 1961.

49. Blumenson, Martin. "D-Day in Retrospect: Could the Germans Have Won?" *Army* 14 (June 1964): 69–75.

50. Blumenson, Martin. *Liberation*. Morristown, N.J.: Time-Life Books, 1978.

51. Blumenson, Martin. "The Most Overrated General of World War II." *Armor* 61 (May–June 1962): 4–10.

52. Blumenson, Martin, and James L. Stokesbury. *Masters of the Art of Command*. Boston: Houghton Mifflin, 1975.

53. Blumentritt, Gunther. *Von Rundstedt: The Soldier and the Man*. London: Oldhams, 1952.

54. Boel, Geoff. *The Normandy Nobodies*. London: Blandford, 1988.

55. Bohanan, Robert D. *Dwight D. Eisenhower: A Selected Bibliography of Periodical and Dissertation Literature*. Abilene, Kans.: Eisenhower Library, 1981.

56. Bolland, A. D. *Team Spirit: The Administration of an Infantry Division During "Operation Overlord."* Aldershot, England: Gale & Polden, 1948.

57. Bookman, John T., and Stephen T. Powers. *The March to Victory: A Guide to World War II Battles and Battlefields from London to the Rhine.* New York: Harper & Row, 1986.

58. Botting, Douglas. *The Second Front.* Alexandria, Va.: Time-Life Books, 1978.

59. Bousel, Patrice. *D-Day Beaches Revisited.* London: MacDonald, 1966.

60. Bovee, D. E. "Hedgerow Fighting." *Infantry Journal* 4 (October 1944): 8–18.

61. Bowyer, Michael J. F. *2nd Group R.A.F.—A Complete History, 1936–1945.* London: Faber, 1974.

62. Boyd, Carl. "Significance of MAGIC and the Japanese Ambassador to Berlin: (V) News of Hitler's Defense Preparations for Allied Invasion of Western Europe." *Intelligence and National Security* 4, no. 2 (1989): 461–81.

63. Bradley, Omar N. *A Soldier's Story.* New York: Henry Holt, 1951.

64. Bradley, Omar N., and Clay Blair. *A General's Life.* New York: Simon & Schuster, 1983.

65. Brendon, Piers. *Ike: His Life and Times.* New York: Harper & Row, 1986.

66. Brereton, Lewis H. *The Brereton Diaries.* New York: William Morrow, 1946.

67. Breuer, William B. *Hitler's Fortress Cherbourg: The Conquest of a Bastion.* New York: Stein & Day, 1984.

68. Brookes, Andrew J. *Photo Reconnaissance.* London: Ian Allan, 1975.

69. Brooks, Stephen. *Operation Overlord*. Southampton, England: Ashford, 1989.

70. Brooks, Stephen. "Montgomery and the Preparation for Overlord." *History Today* 34 (June 1984): 18–22.

71. Brown, Anthony Cave. *Bodyguard of Lies*. New York: Harper & Row, 1975.

72. Brown, Ashley, and Jonathon Reed, eds. *The Armour*. Harrisburg, Pa.: The National History Society, 1986.

73. Browne, A. T. A. "A Study of the Anatomy of Fear and Courage in War." *The Army Quarterly and Defence Journal* 106, no. 3 (July 1976): 297–303.

74. Browne, Archie. "The Breakout from the Normandy Bridgehead, August 1944." *The Army Quarterly and Defence Journal* 112, no. 3 (1982): 338–46.

75. Brownlowe, L. C. *The Mulberry Project*. London: Chatto and Windus, 1957.

76. Bryant, Sir Arthur, ed. *The Alanbrooke War Diaries*. Vol. I. *The Turn of the Tide*. Vol. II. *Triumph in the West*. London: Collins, 1957, 1959.

77. Buell, Thomas B. *Master of Sea Power: A Biography of Fleet Admiral Ernest J. King*. Boston: Little, Brown, 1980.

78. Burgett, Donald. *Currahee! "We Stand Alone!" A Paratrooper's Account of the Normandy Invasion*. New York: Hutchinson, 1967.

79. Bush, Vannevar. *Pieces of the Action*. New York: Morrow, 1970.

80. Butcher, Harry C. *My Three Years with Eisenhower: The Personal Diary of Captain Harry C. Butcher*. New York: Simon & Schuster, 1946.

81. Butler, J. M. A. *Grand Strategy*. Vol. III, Part II. London: H.M. Stationary Office, 1957.

82. Button, Robert E. "Ultra sur le theatre Europeen." *Revue d'Histoire de la Deuxieme Guerre Mondiale et des Conflits Contemporains* 34 (1984): 43–52.

83. Carell, Paul Karl. *Invasion—They're Coming! The German Account of the Allied Landings and the 80 Days' Battle for France*. London: Harrap, 1962.

84. Carrington, Charles. *Soldier at Bomber Command*. London: Leo Cooper, 1987.

85. Casey, Robert J. *This Is Where I Came In*. New York: Bobbs-Merrill, 1945.

86. Cawthon, Charles R. "July, 1944: St. Lô." *American Heritage* 25, no. 4 (June 1974): 4–11, 82+.

87. Cawthon, Charles R. *Other Clay: A Remembrance of the World War II Infantry*. Niwot, Colo.: University Press of Colorado, 1990.

88. Cawthon, Charles R. "Pursuit: Normandy, 1944, An Infantryman Remembers How It Was." *American Heritage* 29, no. 2 (February/March 1978): 80–91.

89. Chalmers, William S. *Full Cycle: The Biography of Admiral Sir Bertram Ramsay*. London: Hodder & Stoughton, 1950.

90. Chancellor, John. "From Normandy to Grenada." *American Heritage* 36 (1985): 32–33.

91. Chandler, Alfred D., Jr. *The Papers of Dwight David Eisenhower. Vol. III. The War Years*. Baltimore: The Johns Hopkins Press, 1970.

92. Chant, Christopher. *The Encyclopedia of Code Names of World War II*. London: Routledge, 1986.

93. Chant, Christopher. *Ground Attack*. London: Almark, 1976.

94. Cherniss, Ruth. "St. Lô: The Resurrection of a Dead City." *Saturday Review of Literature* 3 (July 5, 1969): 11-15+.

95. Chevallier-Appert, Claude. "Overlord." *Revue des Deux Mondes* 9 (1984): 594-98.

96. Christman, Calvin L., and Dennis Showalter. "Doctoral Dissertations in Military Affairs." Annual Series Supplement. MILLAFF, 37-52 (1973-1988).

97. Churchill, Winston S. *The Second World War*. 6 vols. Boston and London: Houghton Mifflin, 1948-1953, 1959.

98. Clay, Ewart W. *The Path of the 50th: The Story of the 50th (Northumbrian) Division in the Second World War, 1939-1945*. Aldershot, England: Gale & Polden, 1950.

99. Cline, Ray S. *Washington Command Post: The Operations Division*. U.S. Army in World War II. Washington, D.C.: Government Printing Office, 1951.

100. Coker, Coit N. "Fire Control on Omaha Beach." *Field Artillery Journal* 36 (September 1946): 530-33.

101. Coletta, Paolo. *A Bibliography of American Naval History*. Annapolis: U.S. Naval Institute Press, 1981.

102. Coll, Blanche D., et al. *The Corps of Engineers: Troops and Equipment. U.S. Army in World War II: The Technical Services*. Washington, D.C.: Office of the Chief of Military History Department of the Army, 1958.

103. Collins, J. Lawton. *Lightning Joe*. Baton Rouge: Louisiana State University Press, 1979.

104. Columbia Broadcasting System. *From D-Day Through Victory in Europe: The Eyewitness Story as Told by War Correspondents on the Air*. New York: CBS, 1945.

105. Combaux, E. "Le BCRA et l'Operation Overlord." *Defense National* (France) 38 (June 1982): 73–85.

106. Cooke, O. A. *The Canadian Military Experience, 1867–1983: A Bibliography.* 2d ed. Ottawa: Canadian Government Publishing Centre, 1984.

107. Cooper, John. *Invasion, the D-Day Story.* London: Beaverbrook Newspapers, 1954.

108. Cooper, Matthew. *The German Army, 1939–1945: Its Political and Military Failure.* London: Macdonald and Janes, 1978.

109. Copp, Terry, and Bill McAndrew. *Battle Exhaustion: Soldiers and Psychiatrists in the Canadian Army, 1939–1945.* Montreal: McGill Queen's University Press, 1990.

110. Courtney, W. B. "The 100 Hours." *Collier's* (August 12, 1944): 11+.

111. Covington, Henry L. *A Fighting Heart: An Unofficial Story of the 82nd Airborne.* Fayetteville, N.C.: Privately printed, 1949.

112. Craven, Wesley Frank, and James L. Cate, eds. *The Army Air Forces in World War II, Vol. III, Europe: Argument to V-E Day, January 1944 to May 1945.* Chicago: University of Chicago Press, 1951. Washington, D.C.: Office of A. F. History, 1983.

113. Critchell, Lawrence. "Air Drop in Normandy." In Frank Brookhauser, ed., *This Was Your War: An Anthology of Great Writings from World War II.* Garden City, N.Y.: Doubleday, 1960.

114. Crookendon, Napier. *Dropzone Normandy: The Story of the British and American Airborne Assault, D-Day 1944.* New York: Scribner's, 1976.

115. Cruickshank, Charles Greig. *Deception in World War II.* London: Oxford University Press, 1979.

116. Cruickshank, Charles Greig. *Strategic and Operational Deception in the Second World War.* London: Frank Cass, 1987.

117. "D-Day Revisited." *National Guard* 38 (September 1984): 12-14+.

118. "D-Day Revisited by Five Who Were There." *Armed Forces Journal* 106, no. 40 (June 7, 1969): 16-18.

119. Dahms, Hellmuth. *Der Zweite Weltkrieg.* Tubingen: R. Wunderlich, 1960, 1965.

120. Dalgleish, John. *We Planned the Second Front.* London: Gollancz, 1945.

121. Daniel, Hawthorne. *For Want of a Nail: The Influence of Logistics on War.* New York: Whittlesey House, 1948.

122. Dank, Milton. *D-Day.* New York: F. Watts, 1984.

123. Dawson, W. Forrest, ed. *Saga of the All American.* Atlanta: Albert Love Enterprises, 1946.

124. Deac, Wilfred P. "Vanguard of Invasion." *British Heritage* (August/September 1989): 34-40.

125. Deborin, G. A. *History of the Great Patriotic War of the Soviet Union, 1941-1945.* 6 vols. Moscow: Military Publishing House, 1960. On microfilm, Wilmington, Del.: Scholarly Resources, 1984.

126. DeGaulle, Charles. *The Complete War Memoirs of Charles DeGaulle.* Translated by Richard Howard. New York: Simon & Schuster, 1960.

127. DeGuingand, Sir Francis. *Operation Victory.* New York: Scribner's, 1947.

128. D'Este, Carlo. *Decision in Normandy.* New York: E. P. Dutton, 1983.

129. *Destination D-Day.* Video Tape. BBC-TV Production, 1984.

130. Detweiler, D. S., et al., eds. *World War II Military Studies.* Vol. 12. *The Western Theater.* New York: Garland, 1972.

131. Deutsch, Harold C. "The Influence of ULTRA on World War II." *Parameters: Journal of U.S. Army War College.* 8, no. 4 (December 1978): 2–15.

132. Doenitz, Karl. *Memoirs: Ten Years and Twenty Days.* London: Weidenfeld & Nicolson, 1958.

133. Dornbusch, Charles E. *Canadian Army, 1855–1965: Lineages, Regimental Histories.* Cornwallville, N.Y.: Hope Farm Press, 1966.

134. Dornbusch, Charles E. *Unit Histories, Personal Narratives, United States Army: A Checklist.* Cornwallville, N.Y.: Hope Farm Press, 1967.

135. Doubler, Michael D. *Busting the Bocage: American Combined Arms Operations in France, 6 June–31 July 1944.* Fort Leavenworth, Kans.: Combat Studies Institute, 1988.

136. Duboscq, Genevieve. *My Longest Night.* New York: Random House, 1981.

137. Dunn, Walter Scott. *Second Front Now, 1943.* Tuscaloosa: University of Alabama Press, 1980.

138. Dunn, William R. *Fighter Pilot: The First American Ace of World War II.* Lexington: The University of Kentucky Press, 1982.

139. Dupuy, R. Ernest, and Trevor N. Dupuy. *The Encyclopedia of Military History: From 3500 B.C. to the Present.* New York: Harper & Row, 1977.

140. Edwards, Kenneth. *Operation Neptune.* London: Collins, 1946.

141. Ehrman, John. *Grand Strategy.* History of the Second World War. United Kingdom Military Series. Vol. V. London: H.M. Stationary Office, 1956.

142. Eisenhower, Dwight D. *Crusade in Europe.* New York: Doubleday, 1948.

143. Eisenhower, Dwight D. *Report by the Supreme Commander to the Combined Chiefs of Staff on the Operations in Europe of the Allied Expeditionary Force, 6 June 1944 to 8 May 1945.*

144. Eisenhower, John. *Allies: Pearl Harbor to D-Day.* New York: Doubleday, 1982.

145. Eisenhower, John. "Eisenhower: 46 Years Ago In Life (Dwight D. Eisenhower)." *Life* 13 (June 1990): 118.

146. Eisenhower Foundation. *D-Day: The Normandy Invasion in Retrospect.* Lawrence: University Press of Kansas, 1971.

147. Eisenhower Interview. *U.S. News and World Report.* 28, no. 5 (February 3, 1950).

148. Eldredge, H. Wentworth. "Biggest Hoax of the War. Operation FORTITUDE: The Allied Deception Plan That Fooled the Germans about Normandy." *Air Power History* 37 (Fall 1990): 15–22.

149. Ellis, John. *Brute Force: Allied Strategy and Tactics in the Second World War.* New York: Viking, 1990.

150. Ellis, L. F. *Victory in the West: The Battle of Normandy.* Vol. 1. History of the Second World War. London: H.M. Stationary Office, 1962.

151. Ellsberg, Edward. *The Far Shore.* New York: Dodd, Mead, 1960.

152. Embry, Sir Basil. *Mission Completed.* London: Methuen, 1957.

153. English, John A. *The Canadian Army and the Normandy Campaign: A Study of Failure in High Command.* New York: Praeger, 1991.

154. Enser, A. G. S. *A Subject Bibliography of the Second World War: Books in English, 1939–1974.* Boulder, Colo.: Westview, 1977.

155. Enser, A. G. S. *A Subject Bibliography of the Second World War: Books in English, 1975–1983.* Brookfield, Vt.: Gower Publishing Co., 1985.

156. Esposito, Vincent J. *The West Point Atlas of American Wars. Vol. II, 1900–1953.* New York: Frederick A. Praeger, 1959.

157. Essame, H. *Normandy Bridgehead.* New York: Ballantine, 1970.

158. Ewing, Joseph H. *Twenty-Nine Let's Go! A History of the 29th Infantry Division in World War II.* Washington, D.C.: Infantry Journal Press, 1948.

159. Falk, Colonel Stanley L. "D-Day + 45 years: A City Remembers." *Army* 39, no. 6 (June 1989): 50–53+.

160. Feasby, W. R., ed. *Organization and Campaigns.* In the series, Official History of the Canadian Medical Services, 1939–1945. Ottawa: Minister of National Defense, 1956.

161. Fergusson, Bernard. *The Watery Maze: The Story of Combined Operations.* New York: Holt, Rinehart and Winston, 1961.

162. First U.S. Army. *Report of Operations.* Printed in Europe, 1946.

163. Fisher, Richard. *With the French Minesweepers.* London: Selwyn and Blount, 1945.

164. Florentin, Eddy. "40eme Anniversaire du Debarquement: Les Cinq Heures H Du Jour." *Historama* 4 (1984): 68–77.

165. Florentin, Eddy. "Les Revelations du General Sir Nigel Poett: Coup de Main sur le Pont Pegase." *Historama* 31 (1986): 42–47.

166. Foot, M. R. D. *SOE in France: An Account of the Work of the British Special Operations Executive in France, 1940–1944.* London: H.M. Stationary Office, 1966.

167. *Foreign Relations of the United States: The Conferences at Washington and Quebec, 1943.* Washington, D.C.: Government Printing Office, 1970.

168. Forester, C. S. "History's Biggest Gamble." *The Saturday Evening Post* (August 12, 1944): 18+.

169. Fouilloux, Etienne. " 'Memoires' Du Debarquement En Normandie." *Annales de Normandie* 36 (1986): 105–19.

170. Fowler, John G. "Command Decision." *Military Review* 59, no. 6 (June 1979): 2–6.

171. Frank, Anne. *The Diary of a Young Girl.* Garden City, N.Y.: Doubleday, 1952.

172. Freidin, Seymour, and William Richardson, eds. *The Fatal Decisions.* New York: Sloane Associates, 1956.

173. Fry, Michael. "Mulberry Harbors." *British History* 1, no. 4 (1974): 2–15.

174. Funk, Arthur Layton, ed. *The Second World War: A Select Bibliography of Books in English Since 1975.* Claremont, Calif.: Regina, 1985.

175. Fussell, Paul. *Wartime: Understanding and Behavior in the Second World War.* New York: Oxford University Press, 1989.

176. Futter, Geoffrey. *The Funnies: A History, with Scale Plans of the 79th Armoured Division.* Hemel Hempstead, Hertfordshire: Clarks, Doble, and Brendon, 1974.

177. Gabel, Christopher R. "Books on Overlord: A Select Bibliography and Research Agenda on the Normandy Campaign, 1944." *Military Affairs* 48 (July 1984): 144–48.

178. Gale, Sir Richard N. *Call to Arms: An Autobiography.* London: Hutchinson, 1968.

179. Gale, Sir Richard N. *With the 6th Airborne Division in Normandy.* London: Low, Marston, 1948.

180. Garth, David, and Charles H. Taylor. *St. Lô (7 July–19 July 1944).* American Forces in Action. Washington, D.C.: Historical Division, War Department, 1946, 1984.

181. Gaskill, Gordon. "Bloody Beach: The Assault on Normandy." *American Magazine* 138 (September 1944): 26–27+.

182. Gavin, James M. *On to Berlin: Battles of an Airborne Commander, 1943–1946.* New York: Viking, 1978.

183. Gavin, James M. "Back Door to Normandy." *Infantry Journal* 63 (November 1946): 9–19.

184. Gilbert, Martin. *Winston S. Churchill. Vol. VII, Road to Victory, 1941–1945.* Boston: Houghton Mifflin, 1986.

185. Glassman, Henry S. *"Lead the Way Rangers": The Fifth Ranger Battalion.* Nashville, Tenn.: Battery Press, 1980.

186. Gleeson, James, and Tom Waldron. *Now It Can Be Told.* London: Paul Elek, 1951.

187. Godson, Susan H. *Viking of Assault: Admiral John Leslie Hall, Jr., and Amphibious Warfare.* Washington, D.C.: University Press of America, 1982.

188. Goerlitz, W. *Memoirs of Field Marshal Wilhelm Keitel.* London: William Kimber, 1965.

189. Golley, John. *The Big Drop: The Guns of Merville, June 1944.* London: Jane's, 1982.

190. Golley, John. *The Day of the Typhoon: Flying with the RAF Tankbusters in Normandy.* Cambridge: Patrick Stephens, 1986.

191. Graham, Smith. *When Jim Crow Met John Bull: Black American Soldiers in World War II Britain.* New York: St. Martin's, 1987.

192. Granatstein, J. L. *Bloody Victory: Canadians and the D-Day Campaign, 1944.* Toronto, Ont.: Lester & Orpen Dennys, 1984.

193. Green, Constance M., Harry C. Thomson, and Peter C. Roots. *The Ordnance Dept: Planning Munitions for War. U.S. Army in World War II: The Technical Services.* Washington, D.C.: Office of the Chief of Military History Department of the Army, 1955.

194. Greene, Ralph C. "What Happened Off Devon?" *American Heritage* 36 (1985): 26–35.

195. Greenfield, Kent Roberts. *American Strategy in World War II: A Reconsideration.* Baltimore: Johns Hopkins Press, 1963.

196. Greenfield, Kent Roberts. *Command Decisions.* New York: Harcourt Brace, 1959.

197. Grigg, John. *1943: The Victory That Never Was.* New York: Hill & Wang, 1980.

198. Guingand, Sir Francis de. *Operation Victory.* London: Hodder & Stoughton, 1947.

199. Guttman, Jon S. "The 29th 'Blue and Gray' Infantry Division: Fighting through the Hedgerows to St. Lô." *National Guard* 44 (September 1990): 48–51.

200. Hall, H. D. *North American Supply.* London: H.M. Stationary Office, 1955.

201. Hall, H. D., and C. C. Wrigley. *Studies in Overseas Supply.* London: H.M. Stationary Office, 1956.

202. Hallion, Richard P. "Battlefield Air Support: A Retrospective Assessment." *Airpower Journal* 4, no. 1 (Spring 1990).

203. Hallion, Richard P. *Strike from the Sky: The History of Battlefield Air Attack, 1911–1945.* Washington, D.C.: Smithsonian Institution Press, 1989.

204. Halloran, Richard. "Soldiers and Scribblers Revisited: Working with the Media." *Parameters* (Spring 1991): 10–14.

205. Hamilton, Nigel. *Master of the Battlefield: Monty's War Years, 1942–1944.* New York: McGraw Hill, 1983.

206. Hammond, William M. *Overlord: The Normandy Invasion from the Landing to St. Lô.* Forthcoming publication by the U.S. Army Center of Military History, 1994.

207. Hansell, Haywood S., Jr. *The Air Plan That Defeated Hitler.* Atlanta, Ga.: Higgins-McArthur, 1972.

208. Hargrove, Charles. "Quarante Ans Apres." *Revue des Deux Mondes* 7 (1984): 104–11.

209. Harris, Sir Arthur. *Bomber Offensive.* London: Collins, 1947.

210. Harris, Dennis E. "The Diplomacy of the Second Front: America, Britain, Russia and the Normandy Invasion." Ph.D. diss., University of California, Santa Barbara, 1969.

211. Harrison, Gordon A. "Airborne Assault in Normandy." *Military Review* 29 (July 1949): 8–22.

212. Harrison, Gordon A. *Cross-Channel Attack.* U.S. Army in World War II: The European Theater of Operations. Washington, D.C.: Government Printing Office, 1951.

213. Hartcup, Guy. *Camouflage: A History of Concealment and Deception in War.* New York: Scribner, 1980.

214. Hartcup, Guy. *Code Name Mulberry: The Planning, Building, and Operation of the Normandy Harbours.* Newton Abbot: David & Charles; New York: Hippocrene, 1977.

215. Hastings, Max. *Das Reich: The March of the 2nd SS Panzer Division through France.* New York: Holt, Rinehart and Winston, 1982.

216. Hastings, Max. *Overlord: D-Day and the Battle of Normandy.* New York: Simon & Schuster, 1984.

217. Hastings, Max. *Victory in Europe: D-Day to V-E Day.* Photographs by George Stevens. Boston: Little, Brown, 1985.

218. Haswell, Jock. *D-Day: Intelligence and Deception.* New York: Times Books, 1979.

219. Hatch, Gardner N., ed. *4th Infantry "Ivy" Division.* Paducah, Ky.: Turner, 1987.

220. Hawkins, Desmond, ed. *War Report: A Record of Dispatches Broadcast by the BBC's War Correspondents with the Allied Expeditionary Force, 6 June 1944–5 May 1945.* London and New York: Oxford University Press, 1946.

221. Hayn, Friedrich. *Die Invasion—Von Contentin bis Falaise.* Heidelberg: Kurt Vowinckel Verlag.

222. Heavey, William F. *Down Ramp! The Story of the Army Amphibian Engineers.* Washington, D.C.: Infantry Journal Press, 1947.

223. Helmdach, F. "Invasion in Frankreich in June 1944." *Allgem. Schweizer Militarzeitschrift* 140 (1974).

224. Hemingway, Ernest. "Voyage to Victory." *Collier's* (July 22, 1944): 11, 56–57.

225. Hesketh, Roger F. *"Fortitude": A History of Strategic Deception in North Western Europe, April 1943 to May 1945.* London: H.M. Stationary Office, 1979.

226. Hewitt, Robert L. *Work Horse of the Western Front: The Story of the 30th Infantry Division.* Washington, D.C.: Infantry Journal Press, 1946.

227. Hickling, Harold. *Sailor at Sea.* London: Kimber, 1965.

228. Higgins, Edward T. *Webfooted Warriors: The Story of a "Frogman" in the Navy During World War II.* New York: Exposition Press, 1955.

229. Higgins, Trumbull. *Winston Churchill and the Second Front.* New York: Oxford University Press, 1957.

230. Higham, Robin. *A Guide to the Sources in American Military History.* Hamden, Conn.: Archon Books, 1975.

231. Higham, Robin. *A Guide to the Sources in British Military History.* Berkeley: University of California Press, 1971.

232. Hine, Al. *D-Day: The Invasion of Europe.* New York: American Heritage, 1962.

233. Hinsley, F. H. *British Intelligence in the Second World War. Its Influence on Strategy and Operations.* Vol. III, Part II. New York: Cambridge University Press, 1988.

234. Holman, Gordon. *Stand By to Beach.* London: Hodder & Stoughton, 1944.

235. Holmes, K. S. *Operation Overlord . . . History of the Work of the Army Postal Services in Relation to Overlord.* London: Powage Press, 1984.

236. Holt, Tonie, and Valmai Holt. *The Visitor's Guide to Normandy Landing Beaches, Memorials and Museums.* Edison, N.J.: Hunter Publishing, Inc., 1989.

237. Hooper, N. John. "Viewpoints on Europe: D-Day Remembered: Legends and Legacies." *Military Review* 66 (June 1986): 50–56.

238. Hoopes, Roy. *Ralph Ingersoll, A Biography.* New York: Atheneum, 1985.

239. Horrocks, Sir Brian. *Corps Commander.* London: Magnum, 1979.

240. How, J. J. *Normandy: The British Breakout.* London: William Kimber, 1981.

241. Howard, Michael. "The Battle of Normandy." *The Listener* 69 (February 21, 1963): 329–31.

242. Howard, Michael. "The Field-Marshal." *New Statesman* (November 8, 1958): 643–44.

243. Howard, Michael. *Grand Strategy.* Vol. IV. London: H.M. Stationary Office, 1972.

244. Howard, Michael. *The Mediterranean Strategy in the Second World War.* London: Weidenfield and Nicolson, 1968.

245. Howarth, David A. *D-Day, the 6th of June, 1944.* New York: McGraw-Hill, 1959.

246. Hoyt, Edwin Palmer. *The GI's War: The Story of American Soldiers in Europe in World War II.* New York: McGraw-Hill, 1989.

247. Hoyt, Edwin Palmer. *The Invasion Before Normandy: The Secret Battle of Slapton Sands.* New York: Stein and Day, 1985.

248. Hunt, Robert, and David Mason. *Camera at War: The Normandy Campaign Leo Cooper.* London: Leo Cooper, 1976.

249. Hunter, Kenneth E. *The War Against Germany: Europe and Adjacent Areas.* Washington, D.C.: Government Printing Office, 1951. The "Green Book" pictorial history of the Army in ETO.

250. Huston, James A. *Out of the Blue: U.S. Army Airborne Operations in World War II.* West Lafayette, Ind.: Purdue University Press, 1972.

251. Ingersoll, Ralph. *Top Secret*. New York: Harcourt Brace, 1946.

252. Irving, David. *The War Between the Generals*. London: Allen Lane, 1981.

253. Ismay, Lord. *Memoirs*. New York: Viking, 1960.

254. Jackson, William G. F. *"Overlord": Normandy 1944*. London: Davis-Poyter, 1978.

255. Jacobsen, H. A., and J. Rohwer, eds. *Decisive Battles of World War II: The German View*. New York: Putnam's, 1965.

256. Jefferson, Alan. *Assault on the Guns of Merville*. London: Murray, 1987.

257. Johns, Glover S., Jr. *The Clay Pigeons of St. Lô*. New York: Bantam, 1985.

258. Johnson, Gerden F. *History of the Twelfth Infantry Regiment in World War II*. Boston: Privately printed, 1947.

259. Jones, R. V. *Most Secret War*. (Alternate title: *The Wizard War: British Scientific Intelligence, 1919–1945*.) London: Hamish Hamilton, 1978.

260. Jonson, Garry, and Christopher Dunphie. *Brightly Shone the Dawn*. London: Warne, 1980.

261. Jordan, Gerald. *British Military History: A Supplement to Robin Higham's Guide to the Sources*. New York: Garland, 1988.

262. Kahn, David. *Hitler's Spies: German Military Intelligence in World War II*. New York: Macmillan, 1978.

263. Karig, Walter. *Battle Report*. Vol. II, *The Atlantic War*. New York: Rinehart, 1946.

264. Karig, Walter. "Rhinos and Mulberries." *United States Naval Institute Proceedings* 71 (December 1945): 1415–25.

265. Kedward, H. R. *Resistance in Vichy France.* Oxford: Oxford University Press, 1978.

266. Keegan, John. *Encyclopedia of World War II.* London: Hamlyn, 1977.

267. Keegan, John. "Normandy and Aftermath." *History Today* 34 (July 1984): 31–35.

268. Keegan, John. *The Second World War.* London: Century Hutchinson, 1989.

269. Keegan, John. *Six Armies in Normandy: From D-Day to the Liberation of Paris, June 6th–August 25th, 1944.* New York: Viking, 1982.

270. Keegan, John, ed. *The Times Atlas of the Second World War.* New York: Harper & Row, 1989.

271. Keegan, John, and Catherine Bradley. *Who Was Who in World War II.* New York: Crowell, 1978.

272. Kelly, John M. "Night the Ground Shook." *Combat Crew* 36 (August 1986): 8–10.

273. Kennett, Lee B. *G. I.: The American Soldier in World War II.* New York: Scribner, 1987.

274. Keyssar, Helene, and Vladimir Pozner. *Remembering War: A U.S.-Soviet Dialogue.* New York: Oxford University Press, 1990.

275. Kimball, Warren F. *Churchill and Roosevelt: The Complete Correspondence.* Princeton, N.J.: Princeton University Press, 1984.

276. Kindleberger, Charles P. "A Rejoinder." *Encounter* 3, no. 6 (June 1979): 89.

277. Kindleberger, Charles P. "Zuckerman's Bomb: World War II Strategy." *Encounter* 51, no. 5 (November 1978): 39–42.

278.   King, Ernest J., and W. M. Whitehill. *Fleet Admiral King: A Naval Record.* New York: Norton, 1952.

279.   Kingston McCloughry, E. J. *The Direction of War: A Critique of the Political Direction and High Command in War.* New York: Frederick A. Praeger, 1955.

280.   Knickerbocker, H. R., et al. *Danger Forward: The Story of the First Division in World War II.* Washington, D.C.: Society of the First Division, 1947.

281.   Koskimaki, George E. *D-Day with the Screaming Eagles.* New York: Vantage, 1970.

282.   Kuhn, Volkmar. *German Paratroopers in World War Two.* London: Ian Allen, 1974.

283.   Kurowski, Franz. *Die Panzer Lehr Division.* Bad Neuheim: Podzun, 1964.

284.   Ladd, James. *Commandos and Rangers of World War Two.* New York: St. Martin's Press, 1978.

285.   Lamb, Richard. *Montgomery in Europe 1943–1945. Success or Failure?* London: Buchan & Enright, 1983.

286.   Lampe, David. *Pyke: The Unknown Genius.* London: Evans Brothers, 1959.

287.   Lanchbery, Edward. *Against the Sun: The Story of Wing Commander Roland Beamont.* London: Cassell, 1955.

288.   Lane, Ronald L. *Rudder's Rangers.* Manassas, Va.: Ranger Associates, 1979.

289.   Leahy, William D. *I Was There: The Personal Story of the Chief of Staff to Presidents Roosevelt and Truman, Based on His Notes and Diaries Made at the Time.* New York: Whittlesay House, 1950.

290.   Leckie, Robert. *Delivered from Evil: The Saga of World War II.* New York: Harper & Row, 1988.

291. Lee, Ulysses. *The Employment of Negro Troops.* U.S. Army in World War II. Washington, D.C.: Government Printing Office, 1966.

292. LeGoyet, Colonel Pierre. *Les Grandes Unités Francaises de la Guerre 1939–1945: Historiques Succincts.* Vols. V and VI. Paris: Imprimerie Nationale, 1967–75.

293. Leigh-Mallory, Trafford. "Air Operations by the A.E.A.F. in N.W. Europe from 15 Nov., 1943 to 30 September 1944." *Royal Air Force Quarterly* 18, no. 4 (October 1947).

294. Leighton, Richard M., "Overlord Revisited: An Interpretation of American Strategy in the European War, 1942–1944." *The American Historical Review* 68 (July 1963): 919–37.

295. Leighton, R. M., and R. W. Coakley. *Global Logistics and Strategy, 1940–1943.* Washington, D.C.: Department of the Army, 1968.

296. Lewin, Ronald. *Ultra Goes to War: The First Account of World War II's Greatest Secret Based on Official Documents.* New York: McGraw-Hill, 1978.

297. Lewis, Nigel. *Channel Firing: The Tragedy of Exercise Tiger.* London: Viking, 1989.

298. Lewis, Robert D. "Pegasus Bridge—Prelude to D-Day." *Special Warfare* 2 (Spring 1989): 42–45.

299. Liddell Hart, B. H. *Defense of the West.* New York: Morrow, 1950.

300. Liddell Hart, B. H. *The German Generals Talk.* New York: Morrow, 1948.

301. Liddell Hart, B. H., ed. *The Rommel Papers.* New York: Harcourt, Brace, 1953.

302. Liddell Hart, B. H. *The Tanks. Vol. II. 1939–1945.* New York: Praeger, 1959.

303. Liebling, A. J. "Cross-Channel Trip." *New Yorker* 20 (July 1-15, 1944): 34–38+.

304. Liebling, A. J. *Normandy Revisited.* New York: Simon & Schuster, 1958.

305. Lindsay, Sir Martin. "The Young and the Brave—Morale in Battle." *Army Quarterly & Defense Journal* 104, no. 4. (July 1974): 464–69.

306. Lochner, Louis P., ed. *The Goebbels Diaries, 1942-1943.* New York: Doubleday, 1948.

307. Loewenheim, Francis J., ed. *Roosevelt and Churchill: Their Secret Wartime Correspondence.* New York: Dutton, 1975.

308. Lovat, Lord. *March Past: A Memoir.* London: Weidenfeld and Nicolson, 1978.

309. Lucas, James, and James Barker. *The Battle of Normandy: The Falaise Gap.* New York: Holmes & Meier, 1978.

310. Luck, Hans von. *Panzer Commander: The Memoirs of Colonel Hans von Luck.* New York: Dell, 1989.

311. Ludewig, J. *Ruckzug des Westheeres von der französischen West—und Sudkuste und die nochmalige Stabilisierung der Westfront.* Ph.D. diss., University of Cologne, 1989.

312. Lummis, Eric T. "D-Day, 6 June 1944: The Truth about 3rd British Division." *The Army Quarterly & Defence Journal* 119 (October 1989): 393–407.

313. Lund, Paul, and Harry Ludlum. *The War of the Landing Craft.* New York: Foulsham, 1976.

314. Luther, Craig W. H. *Blood and Honor: The History of the 12th SS Panzer Division "Hitler Youth." 1943-1945.* San Jose, Calif.: R. James Bender, 1987.

315. MacDonald, B. J. S. *The Trial of Kurt Meyer.* Toronto: Clarke, Irwin & Company, 1954.

316. MacDonald, Charles B. *The Mighty Endeavor: American Armed Forces in the European Theater in World War II.* New York: Oxford University Press, 1969.

317. MacDonald, Charles B. "Slapton Sands: The 'Cover-Up' That Never Was." *Army* 38 (June 1988): 64–67.

318. Mack, Harold L. *The Critical Error of World War II.* Issue Paper No. 81-1. Washington, D.C.: National Defense University, 1981.

319. Macksey, Kenneth J. *Anatomy of a Battle.* New York: Stein and Day, 1974.

320. Macksey, Kenneth J. "Build-up for D-Day: The Balance of Armour." In Bernard Fitzsimons, ed., *Tanks and Weapons of World War II.* New York: Beekman House, 1973.

321. Majdalany, Fred. *The Fall of Fortress Europe.* Garden City, N.Y.: Doubleday, 1968.

322. Manning, John J. "Normandy's Artificial Harbors." *Military Engineer* 36 (December 1944): 388–94.

323. Marrin, Albert. *Overlord: D-Day and the Invasion of Europe.* New York: Atheneum, 1982.

324. Marshall, George C., et al. *The War Reports.* New York: J. B. Lippincott, 1947.

325. Marshall, S. L. A. "First Wave at Omaha Beach." *The Atlantic* 206, no. 5 (November 1960): 67–72.

326. Marshall, S. L. A. *Night Drop: The American Airborne Invasion of Normandy.* Boston: Atlantic Monthly Press, 1962.

327. Martin, H. G. *The History of the Fifteenth Scottish Division, 1939–1945.* Edinburgh: Blackwood, 1948.

328. Mason, David. *Who's Who in World War II.* Boston: Little, Brown, 1978.

329. Masterman, John Cecil. *The Double-Cross System in the War of 1939 to 1945.* New Haven, Conn.: Yale University Press, 1972.

330. Matloff, Maurice, and E. M. Snell. *Strategic Planning for Coalition Warfare.* 2 vols. Washington, D.C.: Department of the Army, 1953–59.

331. Maund, L. E. H. *Assault from the Sea.* London: Methuen, 1949.

332. McBryde, Brenda. *A Nurse's War.* London: Chatto & Windus, 1979.

333. McDougall, Murdoch C. *Swiftly They Struck: The Story of No. 4 Commando.* London: Oldhams, 1957.

334. McElwee, William L. *The Battle for D-Day.* London: Faber and Faber, 1965.

335. McKee, Alexander. *Caen: Anvil of Victory.* London: Souvenir Press, 1985.

336. McKee, Alexander. *Last Round Against Rommel: The Battle of the Normandy Beachhead.* New York: The New American Library, 1964.

337. McMichael, William H. "Journey to Victory." *Soldiers* 45, no. 10 (October 1990): 37–41.

338. McNish, Robin. *Iron Division: The History of the 3rd Division.* London: Ian Allen, 1978.

339. Meitzel, Bernard-George. "Caen-Falaise." *The Canadian Army Journal* 4 (April–June 1950).

340. Menaul, Stewart. "Reflections on D-Day 1944." *Contemporary Review* 244, no. 1421 (June 1984): 303–5.

341. Mendelsohn, John. *Covert Warfare: Basic Deception and the Normandy Invasion.* New York: Garland Publishing, Inc., 1989.

342. Mennel, R. *Die Schlubphase des Zweiten Weltkrieges im Westen.* Osnabrück: Munin Verlag, 1981.

343. Messenger, Charles. *The Commandos.* London: William Kimber, 1985.

344. Meyer, Hubert. *Kriegsgeschichte der 12. SS. Panzer Division "Hitlerjugend."* Osnabrück: Munin Verlag, 1982.

345. Michel, Henri. *The Second World War.* Translated by Douglas Parmee. New York: Praeger, 1975.

346. Michel, Henri, ed. *La Libération de la France.* Paris: ONRS, 1976.

347. Michel, Henri, ed. *Revue d'Histoire de la Deuxieme Guerre Mondiale.* Paris, 1950.

348. Michie, Allan A. *The Invasion of Europe: The Story Behind D-Day.* New York: Dodd, 1964.

349. Millar, C. J., and R. G. Goyle. "A Mission-Oriented Analysis of Operation Goodwood." *British Army Review* 94 (April 1990): 15–24.

350. Miller, Marilyn. *D-Day.* Morristown, N.J.: Silver, 1986.

351. Miller, Merle. *Ike the Soldier: As They Knew Him.* New York: Putnam's, 1987.

352. Millett, Allan R., and B. Franklin Cooling. *Doctoral Dissertations in Military Affairs: A Bibliography.* Manhattan: Kansas State University Library, 1972.

353. Millett, Allan R., and Williamson Murray, eds. *Military Effectiveness.* Vol. 3, *The Second World War.* Boston: Allen and Unwin, 1988.

354. Millis, Walter. *The Last Phase: The Allied Victory in Western Europe.* Boston: Houghton Mifflin, 1946.

355. Mitcham, Samuel W., Jr. *Rommel's Last Battle: The Desert Fox & the Normandy Campaign.* New York: Stein & Day, 1983.

356. Mittelman, Joseph B. *Eight Stars to Victory: A History of the Veteran Ninth U.S. Infantry Division.* Columbus, Ohio: F. J. Heer Printing Company, 1948.

357. Monks, Noel. *Eye-Witness.* London: Frederick Muller, 1955.

358. Montgomery, Bernard Law. *The Memoirs of Field Marshal The Viscount Montgomery of Alamein, K. G.* Cleveland, Ohio: World Publishing, 1958.

359. Montgomery, Bernard Law. *North to the Baltic.* London: Hutchinson, 1947.

360. Moore, William F. "Overlord: The Unnecessary Invasion." Air War College, Air University. Maxwell AFB, Alabama, March 1986.

361. Moorehead, Alan. *Eclipse.* London: Hamish Hamilton, 1945.

362. Moran, Lord. *Churchill: Taken from the Diaries of Lord Moran.* Boston: Houghton Mifflin, 1966.

363. Morgan, Sir Frederick E. *Overture to Overlord.* New York: Doubleday, 1950.

364. Morgan, Kay Summersby. *Past Forgetting.* New York: Simon & Schuster, 1975.

365. Morison, Samuel E. *The Invasion of France and Germany, 1944–1945. History of United States Naval Operations in World War II, Vol. XI.* Boston: Little, Brown, 1962.

366. Nalty, Bernard C. *Strength for the Fight: A History of Black Americans in the Military.* New York: The Free Press, 1986.

367. National Broadcasting Company. *This Is the Story of the Liberation of Europe from the Fall of Rome to Victory—as NBC Newsmen Relayed It by Radio to American Listeners.* New York: NBC, 1945.

368. *Negro Year Book, 1941–1946.* Tuskegee, Ala.: Department of Records and Research, 1944.

369. Neillands, Robin. *The Desert Rats: 7th Armoured Division, 1940–1945.* London: Weidenfeld & Nicolson, 1991.

370. Nelson, James, ed. *A Conversation with Alistair Cooke. General Eisenhower on the Military Churchill.* New York: Norton, 1970.

371. Nicholas, David. *Ernie's War: The Best of Ernie Pyle's World War II Dispatches.* New York: Random House, 1987.

372. Noguères, Henri. *Histoire de la Résistance en France.* 5 vols. Paris: Laffont, 1967–81.

373. Norman, Albert. *Operation Overlord, Design and Reality: The Allied Invasion of Western Europe.* Harrisburg, Pa.: The Military Service Publishing Co., 1952.

374. "Normandy, 1944, 1973." *After the Battle* 1 (1973): 1–40.

375. North, John. *Northwest Europe, 1944–1945: The Achievement of 21st Army Group.* London: H.M. Stationary Office, 1953.

376. Norton, G. C. *The Red Devils.* London: Cox & Wyman.

377. Ose, Dieter. *Entscheidung im Westen, 1944: Der Oberbefehlshaber West Und Die Abwehr Der Alliierten Invasion.* Stuttgart: Deutsche, 1982.

378. Osmanski, Frank A. "The Logistical Planning of Operation Overlord" Part I. *Military Review* 29, no. 9 (December 1949): 31–40; Part II (December 1949): 40–48; 30 Part III (January 1950): 50–62.

379. Pappas, George S. *United States Army Unit Histories.* Carlisle Barracks, Pa.: U.S. Army Military History Institute, 1971.

380. Partridge, Colin. *Hitler's Atlantic Wall.* Guernsey: D. I. Publications, 1976.

381. Pergrin, David E. *First Across the Rhine: The 291st Engineer Combat Battalion in France, Belgium, and Germany.* New York: Atheneum, 1989.

382. Perrault, Gilles. *The Secret of D-Day.* Boston: Little, Brown, 1965.

383. Pfeffer, Colonel Gene J. "Weather and Overlord: Contemporary Lessons." Air War College Research Report No. AU-AWC-85-166, Air University, U.S. Air Force, Maxwell Air Force Base, Alabama, March 1985.

384. Pitt, Barrie, and Frances Pitt. *The Month-By-Month Atlas of World War II.* New York: Summit Books, 1989.

385. Pogue, Forrest C. "General of the Army Omar N. Bradley." In Michael Carver, ed., *War Lords: Military Commanders of the 20th Century.* Boston: Little, Brown, 1976.

386. Pogue, Forrest C. *George C. Marshall: Organizer for Victory, 1943–1945.* New York: Viking, 1973.

387. Pogue, Forrest C. *The Supreme Command.* Washington, D.C.: Government Printing Office, 1978.

388. Prados, John. "Monty's D-Day: The British and the Normandy Invasion." *Strategy and Tactics* 1, no. 2 (1985): 14–24.

389. Price, Alfred. *Aircraft versus Submarine: The Evolution of the Anti-Submarine Aircraft, 1912 to 1972.* Annapolis: Naval Institute Press, 1973.

390. Price, Alfred. "The 3-Inch Rocket: How Effective Was It Against the German Tanks in Normandy?" *The Royal Air Forces Quarterly* 15 (Summer 1975): 127–31.

391. Price, Frank James. *Troy H. Middleton: A Biography.* Baton Rouge: Louisiana State University Press, 1974.

392. Pugsley, W. H. *Saints, Devils, and Ordinary Seamen.* London: Collins, 1945.

393. Putney, Diane T. *Ultra and the Army Air Forces in World War II.* Washington, D.C.: Office of Air Force History, 1987.

394. Pyle, Ernie. *Brave Men.* New York: Henry Holt, 1944.

395. Ramsay, Bertram H. *Report by Allied Naval Commander-in-Chief Expeditionary Force on Operation Neptune.* 3 Vols. London: His Majesty's Stationery Office, 1947.

396. Rapport, Leonard, and Arthur Northwood, Jr. *Rendezvous with Destiny: A History of the 101st Airborne Division.* Greeneville, Tenn.: 101st Airborne Division Association, 1965.

397. Rasor, Eugene L. *British Naval History Since 1815: A Guide to the Literature.* New York: Garland Publishing, Inc., 1990.

398. Reed, Caroline. "D-Day Propaganda." *History Today* 34 (June 1984): 27–30.

399. Reit, Seymour. *Masquerade: The Amazing Camouflage Deceptions of World War II.* London: Hawthorn, 1978.

400. Renaud, Alexandre. *Saint-Mere Eglise: First American Bridgehead in France, 6th June 1944.* Monaco: Pathe', 1964.

401. Richards, D., and H. St. George Saunders. *Royal Air Force, 1939–1945.* Vol. 2. London: H.M. Stationary Office, 1954.

402. Richardson, T. A. "Normandy 1944." *Journal of the Royal Artillery* 117 (September 1990): 26–28.

403. Ridgway, Matthew B. *Soldier: The Memoirs of Matthew B. Ridgway.* New York: Harper, 1956.

404. Rohmer, Richard. *Patton's Gap: An Account of the Battle of Normandy 1944.* New York: Beaufort Books, 1981.

405. Rosengarten, Adolph G., Jr. "With Ultra from Omaha Beach to Weimar" in *Military Affairs* 42, no. 131 (October 1978).

406. Roskill, S. W. *The War at Sea, 1939–1945. Vol. III, Part II, History of the Second World War.* London: H.M. Stationary Office, 1961.

407. Roskill, S. W. *White Ensign: The British Navy at War, 1939–1945.* Annapolis: Naval Institute Press, 1960.

408. Rostow, W. W. *Pre-Invasion Bombing Strategy: General Eisenhower's Decision of March 25, 1944.* Austin: University of Texas Press, 1981.

409. Roy, Reginald H. *1944: The Canadians in Normandy.* Canada: MacMillan of Canada, 1984.

410. Ruge, Friedrich. *Der Zeekrieg: The German Navy's Story, 1939–1945.* Annapolis: Naval Institute Press, 1967.

411. Ruge, Friedrich. "Rommel Before Normandy." *United States Naval Institute Proceedings* 80 (June 1954): 612–19.

412. Ruge, Friedrich. *Rommel in Normandy.* Stuttgart: Koehler Verlag, 1959.

413. Ruge, Friedrich. *Rommel in Normandy.* San Rafael, Calif.: Presidio Press, 1979.

414. Rust, Kenn C. *The 9th Air Force in World War II.* Fallbrook, Calif.: Aero Publishers, 1970.

415. Ruppenthal, Roland G. *Logistical Support of the Armies.* Vol. I. Washington, D.C.: Government Printing Office, 1953.

416. Ruppenthal, Roland G. *Utah Beach to Cherbourg 6 June–27 June 1944*. American Forces in Action. Washington, D.C.: Historical Division, War Department, 1947.

417. Ryan, Cornelius. *The Longest Day: June 6, 1944*. New York: Simon & Schuster, 1959.

418. Rzheshevsky, Oleg. *Operation Overlord: From the History of the Second Front*. Moscow: Novosti Press Agency, 1984.

419. Sainsbury, Keith. "Second Front in 1942—A Strategic Controversy Revisited." *British Journal of International Studies* 4, no. 1 (April 1978): 47–58.

420. Salmud, J. B. *The History of the 51st Highland Division, 1939–1945*. Edinburgh: Blackwood, 1953.

421. Saunders, H. St. George. *The Red Beret*. London: Michael Joseph, 1950.

422. Saunders, H. St. George. *Royal Air Force, 1939–1945. Vol. III, The Fight Is Won*. London: H.M. Stationary Office, 1954.

423. Sawyer, Bickford E., Jr. "The Normandy Campaign from Military and Press Sources." M.A. Thesis, University of Missouri, Columbia, Mo., 1957.

424. Sawyer, John. *D-Day*. London: Landsborough Publications, 1960.

425. Scarfe, Norman. *Assault Division: A History of the 3rd Division from the Invasion of Normandy to the Surrender of Germany*. London: Collins, 1947.

426. Schaufelberger, W. "Overlord: Die Landung der Westalluerten." *Allgem. Schweizer Militarzeitschrift* 150 (1984).

427. Schlight, John. "Elwood R. Quesada: Tac Air Comes of Age." In John L. Frisbee, ed., *Makers of the U.S. Air Force*. Washington, D.C.: Office of Air Force History, 1987.

428. Schoenbrun, David. *Soldiers of the Night.* New York: E.P. Dutton, 1980.

429. Schofield, Brian Betham. *Operation Neptune: Sea Battles in Close-up Series.* Annapolis: Naval Institute Press, 1974.

430. Schramm, P. E. *Die Invasion 1944.* Munchen: Bernard, 1963.

431. Schull, Joseph. *The Far Distant Ships: An Official Account of Canadian Naval Operations in the Second World War.* Ottawa: Edmond Clontier, 1950.

432. Schweppenburg, Geys von. "Reflections on the Invasion." *Military Review* 41 (February 1961): 2–11; 42 (March 1961): 12–21.

433. Sekistov, Colonel V. "Why the Second Front Was Not Opened in 1942." *Soviet Military Review* 8 (August 1972): 50–52.

434. Sherwood, Robert E. *Roosevelt and Hopkins: An Intimate History.* New York: Harper and Row, 1948.

435. Sherwood, Robert E. *The White House Papers of Harry L. Hopkins.* 2 vols. London: Eyre & Spottiswoode, 1948, 1949.

436. Shores, Christopher F. *2nd TAF.* Reading, Berkshire: Oprey, 1970.

437. Showalter, Dennis E. *German Military History, 1648–1982: A Critical Bibliography.* New York: Garland, 1984.

438. Shulman, Milton. *Defeat in the West.* London: Secker & Warburg, 1947.

439. Simpson, B. Mitchell, III. *Admiral Harold R. Stark: Architect of Victory, 1939–1945.* Columbia: University of South Carolina Press, 1989.

440. Sixsmith, E. K. G. *Eisenhower As Military Commander.* New York: Stein and Day, 1972.

441. Slessor, Sir John. *The Central Blue.* London: Cassell, 1956.

442. Slessor, Sir John. *The Central Blue: The Autobiography of Sir John Slessor, Marshal of the RAF.* New York: Praeger, 1957.

443. Smith, Graham. *When Jim Crow Met John Bull: Black American Soldiers in World War II Britain.* New York: Macmillan, 1988.

444. Smith, Myron J., Jr. *Air War Bibliography Series, 1939–1945: English-Language Sources.* 5 vols. Manhattan, Kans.: Military Affairs/Aerospace Historian, 1977–1982.

445. Smith, Myron J., Jr. *The Secret Wars: A Guide to the Sources in English.* 3 vols. Santa Barbara, Calif.: ABC-Clio, 1980.

446. Smith, Myron J., Jr. *World War II: The European and Mediterranean Theaters: An Annotated Bibliography.* Wars of the U.S. Series. New York: Garland, 1984.

447. Smith, Myron J., Jr. *World War II at Sea: A Bibliography of Sources in English.* Vol. I, *The European Theater.* Metuchen, N.J.: The Scarecrow Press, 1976.

448. Smith, R. Harris. *OSS: The Secret History of America's First Central Intelligence Agency.* Berkeley: University of California Press, 1972.

449. Smith, Walter Bedell. *Eisenhower's Six Great Decisions: Europe, 1944–1945.* New York: Longmans, Green, 1956.

450. Snyder, Louis L., ed. *Masterpieces of War Reporting, the Great Moments of World War II.* New York: Julian Messner, 1962.

451. Sollers, Edward G. "The Twilight War: Resistance in France, 1940–1944." *Strategy and Tactics* 4 (1984): 46–48.

452. Somers, Martin. "The Longest Hour in History: The U.S. Destroyer *McCook* in the Normandy Invasion." *Saturday Evening Post* 217 (July 8, 1944): 22+.

453. Somers, Martin. "Right, Hard Rudder! All Hands Below!: The U.S. Battleship *Texas* in the Bombardment of Cherbourg." *Saturday Evening Post* 217 (September 16, 1944): 18–19+.

454. Spaatz, Carl A., and Ira C. Eaker. "Reflections on Overlord." *Air Force Magazine* 57 (June 1974): 66.

455. Speidel, Hans. *Invasion 1944: Rommel and the Normandy Campaign.* Chicago: Henry Regnery, 1950.

456. Stacey, C. P. *The Victory Campaign: The Operations in North-West Europe, 1944–1945.* Vol. III, *Official History of the Canadian Army in the Second World War.* Ottawa: Queen's Printer, 1960.

457. Stagg, J. M. *Forecast for Overlord.* London: Ian Allen, 1971.

458. Stanford, Alfred B. *Force Mulberry: The Planning and Installation of the Artificial Harbor off U.S. Normandy Beaches in World War II.* New York: William Morrow, 1951.

459. Stilwell, Joseph W. *The Stilwell Papers.* (ed. T. H. White). New York: MacDonald, 1949.

460. Stimson, Henry L., and McGeorge Bundy. *On Active Service in Peace and War.* London: Hutchinson, 1955.

461. Stoler, Mark A. " 'The Pacific-First' Alternative in American World War II Strategy." *The International Historical Review* 2, no. 3 (July 1980): 432–52.

462. Stoler, Mark A. *The Politics of the Second Front: American Military Planning and Diplomacy in Coalition Warfare, 1941–1943.* Westport, Conn.: Greenwood Press, 1977.

463. Strachan, Hew. "The British Way in Warfare Revisited." *The Historical Journal* 26, no. 2 (1983): 447–61.

464. Strange, Joseph L. "The British Rejection of 'Operation Sledgehammer': An Alternative Motive." *Military Affairs* 46 (February 1982): 6–14.

465. Strong, Sir Kenneth. *Intelligence at the Top: The Recollections of a British Intelligence Officer.* New York: Doubleday, 1969.

466. Strutton, Bill, and Michael Pearson. *The Secret Invaders.* London: British Book Centre, 1959.

467. Sullivan, John L. "The Botched Air Support of Operation Cobra." *Parameters* 18, no. 1 (March 1988): 97–110.

468. Summersby, Kay. *Eisenhower Was My Boss.* New York: Prentice-Hall, 1948.

469. Summersby, Kay. *Past Forgetting: My Love Affair with Dwight D. Eisenhower.* New York: Simon & Schuster, 1976.

470. Sweet, John T. *Mounting the Threat: The Battle of Bourguebus Ridge.* San Rafael: Presidio, 1978.

471. Taylor, Charles H. *Omaha Beach, 6 June–13 June 1944.* American Forces in Action. Washington, D.C.: Historical Division, War Department, 1945.

472. Taylor, Charles H. *Small Unit Actions.* American Forces in Action. Washington, D.C.: Historical Division, War Department, 1946.

473. Tedder, Sir Arthur. *With Prejudice: The War Memoirs of Marshal of the Royal Air Force Lord Tedder.* Boston: Little, Brown, 1966.

474. Terkel, Studs. *"The Good War": An Oral History of World War Two.* New York: Pantheon Books, 1984.

475. Terraine, John. *A Time for Courage: The Royal Air Force in the European War, 1939–1945.* New York: Macmillan, 1985.

476. Thompson, Kenneth. *H.M.S. "Rodney" at War.* London: Hollis & Carter, 1946.

477. Thompson, Paul. "D-Day on Omaha Beach." *Infantry Journal* 56 (June 1945): 34–48.

478. Thomson, R. W. *D-Day: Spearhead of Invasion.* New York: Ballantine Books, 1968.

479. Tippelskirch, Kurt von. *Die Invasion 1944.* Geschicht des Zuueites Weltkriegs, Bonn, 1956.

480. Tobin, Richard L. *Invasion Journal.* New York: Dutton, 1944.

481. Tooley, Peter. *Operation Quicksilver.* London: Ian Henry, 1988.

482. Treadwell, Mattie E. *The U.S. Army in World War II, Special Studies: The Women's Army Corps.* Washington, D.C.: Government Printing Office, 1954.

483. Trukhanovsky, V. G. *Winston Churchill.* Moscow: Progress Publishers, 1978.

484. Truscott, General Lucien. *Command Decisions.* New York: Dutton, 1954.

485. Tugwell, Maurice. *Airborne to Battle: A History of Airborne Warfare, 1918–1971.* London: William Kimber, 1971.

486. Tunney, Christopher. *A Biographical Dictionary of World War II.* New York: St. Martin's Press, 1972.

487. Turner-Chasteen, Camille. "The Fight of the Marquis." *Strategy and Tactics* 4 (1984): 48–51.

488. Turner, John Frayn. *Invasion 1944: The First Full Story of D-Day in Normandy.* New York: Putnam, 1959.

489. Tute, Warren, John Costello, and Terry Hughes. *D-Day*. New York: Macmillan, 1974.

490. U.S. Army. Corps of Engineers. Special Brigade Group. *Operation Report Neptune, Omaha Beach* . . . History Section, ETOUSA, 1944.

491. Usikov, A. "Normandskaia Desantnaia Operatsiia" (The Normandy Landing). *Voenno-Istoricheskii Zhurnal* 6 (1984): 61–69.

492. Valavielle, Michele de. *D-Day at Utah Beach*. Bayeux: Editions Heimdal, 1976.

493. Van Creveld, Martin. *Fighting Power: German and U.S. Army Performance, 1939–1945*. Westport, Conn.: Greenwood Press, 1982.

494. Van Creveld, Martin. *Supplying War: Logistics from Wallenstein to Patton*. New York: Cambridge University Press, 1977.

495. Verney, G. L. *The Desert Rats: The Story of the 7th Armoured Division*. London: Hutchinson, 1954.

496. Vian, Admiral Philip. *Action This Day: A War Memoir*. London: Muller, 1960.

497. Villa, Brian Loring. "The Atomic Bomb and the Normandy Invasion." In Donald Fleming, ed., *Perspectives in American History*. Vol. XI. Cambridge, Mass.: Harvard University Press, 1978.

498. Warlimont, Walter. *Inside Hitler's Headquarters*. London: Weidenfeld & Nicolson, 1962.

499. Warner, Geoffrey. "The Road to D-Day." *History Today* 34 (June 1984): 10–14.

500.   Warren, Arnold. *Wait for the Wagon: The Story of the Royal Canadian Army Service Corps.* Toronto: McClelland & Stewart, 1961.

501.   Webster, Sir Charles, and Noble Frankland. *The Strategic Air Offensive Against Germany 1939–1945.* Vol. III, *Victory.* Part 5. London: H.M. Stationary Office, 1961.

502.   Wedemeyer, Albert C. "Footnotes to D-Day." *The American Legion Magazine* 106, no. 6 (June 1979): 14–39.

503.   Wedemeyer, Albert C. *Wedemeyer Reports.* New York: Henry Holt, 1958.

504.   Wegmuller, H. *Die Abwehr der Invasion. Die Konzeption des OB West, 1940–1944.* Freiburg: Rombach, 1979.

505.   Weigley, Russell F. *The American Way of War: A History of United States Military Strategy and Policy.* Bloomington, Ind.: University Press, 1977.

506.   Weigley, Russell F. *Eisenhower's Lieutenants: The Campaigns of France and Germany, 1944–1945.* Bloomington: Indiana University Press, 1981.

507.   Weigley, Russell F. *History of the United States Army.* New York: Macmillan, 1968.

508.   Weigley, Russell F. "From the Normandy Beaches to the Falaise-Argentan Pocket: A Critique of Allied Operational Planning in 1944." *Military Review* 70, no. 9 (September 1990): 45–64.

509.   Wernher, Sir Harold. *World War II: Personal Experiences.* Privately printed, 1950.

510.   Wertenbaker, Charles C. *Invasion.* New York: Appleton-Century-Crofts, 1944.

511.   Westphal, Siegfried. *The Fatal Decisions.* London: Michael Joseph, 1956.

512. Westphal, Siegfried. *The German Army in the West*. London: Cassell, 1951.

513. Wheal, Elizabeth-Anne, S. Pope, and J. Taylor. *A Dictionary of the Second World War*. New York: Peter Bedrick Books, 1990.

514. Wheldon, Sir Huw. *Red Berets into Normandy*. London: Jarrold, 1982.

515. White, Arthur S. *A Bibliography of Regimental Histories of the British Army*. London: Society for Army Historical Research, 1965.

516. White, Sir Bruce. *Mulberry*. Privately printed, 1980.

517. White, Theodore H., ed. *The Stilwell Papers*. New York: Schocken Books, 1948.

518. Whiting, Charles. *Bradley*. New York: Ballantine, 1971.

519. Wigglesworth, Sir Philip. "Review of Major Ellis's Victory in the West." *RUSI Journal* (March 1963): 172–73.

520. Willmott, H. P. *The Great Crusade: A New Complete History of the Second World War*. New York: Free Press, 1990.

521. Willmott, H. P. *June 1944*. Poole, Dorset: Blantford Press, 1984.

522. Wilmot, Chester. *The Struggle for Europe*. New York: Harper, 1952.

523. Wilson, Michael, and A. S. L. Robinson. *Coastal Command Leads the Invasion*. New York: Jarrold, 1946.

524. Wilt, Alan F. *The Atlantic Wall: Hitler's Defenses in the West, 1941–1944*. Ames: Iowa State University Press, 1975.

525. Winterbotham, Frederick W. *The "Ultra" Secret*. New York: Harper & Row, 1974.

526. Winton, John. *The War at Sea: The British Navy in World War II: An Anthology of Personal Experience.* New York: Morrow, 1967.

527. Wolf, Thomas H. "D-Day Remembered: A Brief Afterglow of Battle Survived." *Smithsonian* (1984): 132–43.

528. Wolfert, Michael L. *From Acts to Cobra: Evolution of Close Air Support Doctrine in World War II.* Maxwell AFB, Alabama: USAF Command and Staff College, 1988.

529. Wolk, Herman S. "Prelude to D-Day: The Bomber Offensive." *Air Force Magazine* 57 (June 1974): 60–65.

530. Wynn, Humphrey, and Susan Young. *Prelude to Overlord.* Novato, Calif.: Presidio, 1983.

531. Wynn, Neil A. *The Afro-American and the Second World War.* New York: Holmes & Meier, 1976.

532. Young, Peter. *Atlas of the Second World War.* New York: G. P. Putnam's Sons, 1974.

533. Young, Peter. *Great Battles of World War II: D-Day.* Northbrook, Ill.: Quality Books, 1981.

534. Young, Peter. *Storm from the Sea.* Annapolis: Naval Institute Press, 1989.

535. Ziegler, Janet, ed. *World War II: Books in English, 1945–1965.* Stanford, Calif.: Hoover Institution, 1971.

536. Ziegler, Philip. *Mountbatten.* New York: Harper, 1985.

537. Zimmerman, Bodo. "France, 1944." In Seymour Freidin and William Richardson, eds., *The Fatal Decisions.* New York: Sloane, 1956.

538. Zuckerman, Solly. *From Apes to Warlords.* New York: Harper & Row, 1978.

539. Zuckerman, Solly. "Bombs and Illusions in World War II." *Encounter* 52, no. 6 (June 1979): 86–89.

INDEX

United States: forces in Britain, 72; military effectiveness, 102 U.S. Air Force: 8th Air Force, 51, 106, 108; 9th Air Force, 106, 108 U.S. Army, 94-97
—Airborne Divisions: 82nd, 80-81; 101st, 80;
—Combat Engineers, 96
—Corps: V, 83; VII, 95; XIX, 108
—Infantry Divisions: 1st, 84; 4th, 85; 9th, 96, 108; 29th, 84, 95; 30th, 96, 108; 90th, 96
—Navy, 54-56
—Rangers, 80-81
Utah Beach, 85-86

Van Creveld, Martin, 41, 95
Vian, Admiral Philip, 55
Villa, Brian Loring, 23
Villers-Bocage, battle at, 101
von Luck, Hans, 108
von Runstedt, Field Marshal Gerd, Commander in Chief West, 75

Warlimont, General Walter, 76
Warren, Arnold, 41
Webster, Sir Charles, 49
Wedemeyer, Colonel (later

General) Albert C., 25
Wegmuller, H., 92
Weigley, Russell F., 24, 94-95, 99, 109, 112
Wertenbaker, Charles C., 44
Wheldon, Sir Hew, 68
Whitehead, Don, 84
Whiting, Charles, 94
Wigglesworth, Air Marshal Sir Philip, 91
Wilmot, Chester, 20, 97
Willmott, H. P., 93-94, 103
Wilson, Michael, 53
Wilson, Sir Charles (later Lord Moran), 21
Wilt, Alan F., 74
Winterbotham, Frederick, 65
Winton, John, 58
Wittmann, Michael, tank "ace," 101
Wolfert, Major Michael L., 106
Wolk, Herman S., 51
Wynn, Humphrey, 53

Young, Peter, 79

Ziegler, Philip, 32
Zimmerman, Bodo, 75
Zuckerman, Professor Solly (later Lord), and Transportation Plan, 48-51

About the Author

COLIN F. BAXTER is Associate Professor of History at East Tennessee State University. Specializing in military history, he is the author of various journal articles dealing with British military history and World War II.

www.ingramcontent.com/pod-product-compliance
Lightning Source LLC
Chambersburg PA
CBHW060313100426
42812CB00003B/765